Katherine Hines is a missionary who li⟨ ⟩
Everything in her life is centered on pouring out the love of ⟨…⟩
all the children and to all the staff working alongside her in Uganda.
She sees people of all ages the way Jesus sees them. She sees individuals in need of a touch from Christ and in need of another chance. She embodies what Russian novelist Fyodor Dostoevsky wrote: "To love a person means to see him the way God intends him to be." Katherine knows Jesus' good intention for everybody regardless of what their present circumstances are, and she invests herself in making those intentions reality. As you read this book, I trust that you'll experience how exciting life is when we, like Katherine, dare to live with a constant "yes" to Jesus' calling on our lives – no matter how crazy His calling may sound.

Torben Riis Jensen
Missions Pastor, Bear Valley Church, Lakewood, Colorado

I have known Katherine Hines for nearly thirty years. I recruited her as one of my first Sunday School teachers when I served as a children's pastor. At that time, she taught my son, Nate, in her four-year-old class. She told me then she wanted to do something great for our Lord. Later when she went to Uganda to start Hines Ugandan Ministries, I had no doubt her passionate faith would carry her. In the twenty years she has sacrificially served in Kamonkoli, countless children have been provided for and have found faith in Jesus Christ. My wife and I personally support children in her ministry. Through the years, I have led three short-term mission teams to Uganda, and each team was inspired in their faith as their eyes were opened to the extreme poverty in our world. Katherine's remarkable story will inspire and renew your faith.

Pastor Mike Lundberg
Church on the Hill, Montrose, Colorado

I have never met anyone who has worked harder to provide for the orphans, vulnerable children, and the widows. Hines is a woman with integrity whose heart overflows with love for the hurting children and, above all, for our God. She has done a remarkable job of helping and caring with a compassionate heart for the physical, emotional, and spiritual needs of the people. In addition to her tremendous testimony of resisting the African bugs, mosquitos, flies, and the diseases that come with them, she is the girl who never left. I am thrilled to be part of Hines Ugandan Ministries.

Charles Magale
Senior Pastor, Kamonkoli Presbyterian Church
Assistant Director of Hines Ugandan Ministries

I have known Momma Katherine Hines since 1998. Her extensive and great work towards helping orphans and widows in Uganda has been manifest for the last twenty years. I am a beneficiary and highly recommend her book for whoever will be reading it!

Evangelist Nelson Duchu
Founder of Revival Harvest Christian Ministries,
Evangelical Missions International

I came to know Katherine Hines when I was six years old in one of the villages in a place called Kamonkoli, Uganda. Through God's grace, hard work, and the cooperation from the sponsors, I was able to go to school, and I attained my Bachelor's degree in environmental science. Thereafter, I was granted the opportunity to serve these wonderful children as I work for the ministry in the child sponsorship department. I advise, council, guide, and direct these children to make wonderful choices that will help as they face the challenges of the day throughout their lifetime until they go to be with the Creator. My dear brothers and sisters and all well-wishers who will get the opportunity to sell, read, or buy this book, I request you to do one thing for the author. If you can help raise funds for her, please do it; but if not, I kindly request you to pray for her. There are many grains in the field, but the people harvesting are few; therefore, I kindly appeal to you to join hands in the harvest in the jungle. May the blessings of God Almighty, the Father, the Son and the Holy Spirit be with you all.

Dison Bumba
Former sponsored child who is now serving in the ministry

Everyday life and poverty in rural Uganda can prove challenging and void of hope for a future. Children have no guarantee of life beyond each day, as they struggle for basic subsistence and witness disease, corruption, and depravity – circumstances into which they were born. As an overcomer of life-impacting challenges of her own, Katherine Hines answered her calling to reach out to these innocent children and the community of Kamonkoli, Uganda, to give them a future hope through Jesus Christ. Children, once without hope, are overcoming these circumstances, growing up to end the cycle of poverty and despair for their families, and becoming godly leaders for their families, community, and country. Through the pages of this book, Katherine shares her inspiring adventure and the transformed lives of these overcomers.

Cindy Stutheit
Home Office Administrator, Hines Ugandan Ministries

They Call Me
Momma
Katherine

They Call Me Momma Katherine

How One Woman's Brokenness Became Hope for Uganda's Children

KATHERINE HINES
With SHEILA WILKINSON

ANEKO
PRESS

Visit Katherine's website: www.hineskids.org

They Call Me Momma Katherine – Katherine Hines

Copyright © 2016

First edition published 2016

Cover Design: Natalia Hawthorne, BookCoverLabs.com

eBook Icon: Icons Vector/Shutterstock

Written with: Sheila Wilkinson

Editor: Heather Thomas

Printed in the United States of America

Aneko Press – *Our Readers Matter*™

www.anekopress.com

Aneko Press, Life Sentence Publishing, and our logos are trademarks of Life Sentence Publishing, Inc.
203 E. Birch Street
P.O. Box 652
Abbotsford, WI 54405

BIOGRAPHY & AUTOBIOGRAPHY / Religious

Paperback ISBN: 978-1-62245-323-8

eBook ISBN: 978-1-62245-324-5

10 9 8 7 6 5 4 3 2 1

Available where books are sold

Share this book on Facebook:

I dedicate this book to my best Friend, my soul mate, my everything – Jesus Christ, and to all the children He has given me in Uganda. I love you all!

Contents

Dear Lord, hear my prayer and give ear to my words
And know that I care from the depths of my heart
For those without hope and without God.
Please, Lord, consider the children of Uganda.

Oh, God to be feared and yet always near,
The God of all nations and King of all kings,
Fill them with love, some joy and some laughter,
The laughter that comes from thy Holy Spirit.

I know in my heart just how great thou art
And hold dear the truth of thy living words.
I ask you to share them with these precious souls
And guide them from sadness to hope evermore.

Bless these dear children whose hearts have been broken;
Their burdens are heavy, no family consoles them.
They need tender mercy and thy loving power
To come to their bedsides and heal them this hour.

Give them each day a bread everlasting,
Show them the way through hope of salvation.
These children need love to fill up their souls,
So make them complete in your loving arms.

Oh Lord, hear my prayer for the children of Uganda.

Foreword

God calls ordinary people to do extraordinary things through His power and His equipping. Meeting such a person impacts an individual in ways that are beyond description.

My long-time friend, Katherine Hines, is such a woman, and her commitment to the children in Uganda is contagious. Hers is a story of heartache, struggle, sacrifice, and remarkable victory for God's kingdom that will touch your life as it has mine. God gave Katherine a deep love for the children of Africa, especially those in Kamonkoli, Uganda. He made it clear to her that she was not to just visit this village and tell of Jesus but to live in Kamonkoli, showing God's love in practical ways on a daily basis.

Kamonkoli is not a village supported by any of the mission boards, so Katherine was on her own but certainly not by herself. She knows what it is like to be in a strange country, living in a primitive shack, eating unusual food, and drinking local water. She knows what it is like to hear a variety of languages and look different from everyone else. She knows what it is like for people to be suspicious of her and at the same time curious about her. She knows the difference between being lonely and being alone.

Katherine embraced the words of Jesus in Matthew 16:24 with joy, Whoever wants to be my disciple must deny themselves and take up their cross and follow me. Jesus led her to sell all that she had, leave her family, friends, and all that was familiar, travel to the other side of the world, and follow Him.

Her obedience to His call began a journey that would result in children without hope receiving hope through faith in Jesus Christ. Katherine has been able to provide a home with love, nourishing food, and clean water to children with nothing. They receive protective shoes, new clothes, an education that elevates their potential, and medical care that brings spiritual and physical healing.

Through the years, young children, orphaned by AIDS, have become young adults who are now contributing members of Uganda's society. Young men and women with hope and hearts to share their faith and their provisions with others. This remarkable story will inspire you, convict you, and motivate you to follow Jesus wherever and however He leads.

Joy Conaway

Member of Board of Directors for Living Proof Ministries

Introduction

Rarely in life do you get to meet such an amazing person. Heroes are glamorized in movies and books by their capes and super powers. I am thrilled for you to meet a real hero in Katherine Hines.

Katherine didn't leap from a building in a single bound or save a city, per se. She did something far more heroic – she stayed.

It may sound simple to those like me on this side of the ocean, but Katherine's heroic action of "staying" was anything but simple. You see, Katherine "simply" left her family and a prosperous accounting career in Colorado to move to the slums of Kampala, Uganda. She sold her belongings and traveled alone for days by plane, car, and foot. She slept in a tent and eventually graduated to a hut. She battled rats, malaria, dysentery, and tribesmen. The odds were against her, and the mosquitos were a constant antagonist, but she persevered. She stayed.

Two decades ago in Uganda, Katherine battled the unseen forces of disbelief that a "Mzungu," a white person, and woman nonetheless, would survive and stay through it all. Local chatter suggested that it was only a matter of time before she, too, would go back to her "real life."

Now, the nationals and mission teams alike know that her grit, her strength, her compassion, and mostly, her God, are what allowed her to stay. Katherine stayed because love motivated her.

On the long bumpy bus rides from Entebbe to Kampala down dusty, orange-clay roads, my wife, Christi, and I have shared in the stories, joys, struggles, and set-backs of Katherine's life. It is astounding to see God's grace and provision in each disappointment and, sometimes, cliff-hanging moment.

Katherine loves the children of Uganda and has laid down her very life that they would know Christ. She is a courageous woman made in the mold of a modern Mother Teresa. Katherine is a hero without the habit or the cape. She is truly the lady who stayed.

Jerry Haag, Ph.D.

President/CEO, Florida Baptist Children's Homes

I am forever grateful to my parents, Jim and Wilma Hines, who have gone to be with the Lord, not only for showing me abundant love but for teaching me of God's love. I thank my brothers who have also loved me and encouraged me, and I thank my friends who have stood by me all the way, just as my Lord has.

I also thank all the children the Lord has given me, for He has made me a mother to all here in Uganda. Special gratitude to the children I have been blessed to raise as my own, who have given me the inspiration I need, together with Jesus.

Special thanks goes to the staff of Hines Ugandan Ministries – Cindy Stuheit, who is our Home Administrator and good friend, always sticking by me through good and bad; the Board of Directors; Pastor Charles Magale and his wife Judith; Christine Nabagenyi, who is the Child Sponsorship Administrator and good friend; and all the others who have come on this journey and served the Lord with me to make a difference in the lives of children – one child at a time.

The Heart is Where It Begins

How, then, can they call on the one they have not believed in? And how can they believe in the one of whom they have not heard? And how can they hear without someone preaching to them? And how can they preach unless they are sent? As it is written, "How beautiful are the feet of those who bring good news!" Romans 10:14-15

My Lord has kept me through many trials and dangers, as He keeps His promises to all those who belong to Him. His love never fails and He indeed never leaves us or forsakes us. He assures us that *neither death nor life, neither angels nor demons, neither the present nor the future, nor any powers, neither height nor depth, nor anything else in all creation, will be able to separate us from the love of God that is in Christ Jesus our Lord* (Romans 8:38-39). I will never walk alone, because He is ever with me.

The Lord is our refuge in times of trouble. He is the one who truly cares about everything in our lives. He is *a refuge for the oppressed, a stronghold in times of trouble* (Psalm 9:9). His love is more than we can imagine, and it never changes. When you love the Lord with all your heart, soul, mind, and strength, you just want to tell everyone about Him and about His great love for them.

Never doubt that He will give you the desires of your heart, as He says *delight yourself in the Lord and he will give you the desires of your heart* (Psalm 37:4). Sometimes it takes a while to learn what the desires of our hearts are. I always wanted to be a mother. I love children and I hate to see them mistreated or abused in any way. The Lord put this in my heart long ago, and He knows what makes us happy. The closer we grow to Him, the closer our purpose will align with His, and we desire to do what He would have us to do.

Like a candle in the dark, I want to shine before all the people the Lord puts in my life, because all over the world, people need the Lord. I desire and want to give Him glory and honor all the days and every moment of my life. One person can make a difference if we are willing to die to self through the power of the Holy Spirit. We can light God's fire in others when the Lord is lighting us.

We are therefore Christ's ambassadors, as though God were making his appeal through us (2 Corinthians 5:20). We are to be a shining light, working for the Lord, examples for Christ to the little children. James 1:27 says that a perfect religion *looks after orphans and widows in their distress.* The children of Uganda and other sub-Saharan countries of Africa suffer. They need a light in their lives. They need the love of Jesus to comfort them, guide them, help them, and provide for them. They need people who are willing to be like big brothers, sisters, or parents to guide and nurture them in love, the love that Jesus gives us so freely. The Lord calls people like you and me to serve Him by helping others find the hope we have found in Him. We are His ambassadors to serve Him by caring for them.

In the song "Who Will Save the Children?" the singer speaks about children who are suffering – children whose dreams are crushed before they begin. It is a cry for all the innocent ones, born into a world that has lost its heart. I have seen this in many different places, but even more in Uganda. These children suffer without food, clothes, and education, but beyond these basic needs, they suffer even more without someone who cares for them and loves them, as they deserve. My heart has come from the Lord Jesus Christ who said to *let the little children come* (Matthew 19:14). The song continues to say, "we shake our fists at the air and say, 'if God is love, how can this be fair?' but . . . we are the ones who must make the choice."[1] We are the ones God wants to use us to make the difference. It takes faith and trust in the Lord, but it is only possible if we are willing to die to ourselves and give of ourselves, letting God take us on a journey that only He can.

I share these stories of what God has done and is doing. How He took me to Uganda and has used me, a nobody, but somebody to Him. I hope to encourage others to follow their dreams in Christ and know that all things are possible with Him. May all who read this book not hold back or be afraid; the door is open for other laborers. Go and make a difference wherever the Lord is leading you, whether at school, work, in the neighborhood, or around the world. We have work to do for our Lord.

This is my story . . . Katherine

---

1   Compassion International asked Randy Stonehill to write them a theme song. The result was "Who Will Save the Children?"

Chapter One

Comfort Out of Suffering

I have told you these things, so that in me you may have peace. In this world you will have trouble. But take heart! I have overcome the world. John 16:33

Trouble. Yes, I had already seen enough trouble to last a lifetime, for I had struggled and grappled with the painful events of my early years and resisted and wrestled with the God who loved me as His own. Now, at 6:30 a.m. in June of 1994, as British Airways delivered me to Entebbe, Uganda, I was immediately struck with the large letters E-N-T-E-B-B-E against the hill at the airport. I grabbed my camera and took aim, but suddenly, a man in a security uniform and carrying an AK-47, approached me and growled, "You are not to take pictures here. Move on please."

I was frightened but did not want to show it, so I turned and continued into the airport. As I came out of the baggage claim with suitcases, I saw a very dark Ugandan man wearing a dress shirt, vest, and trousers (not jeans), and coming my way. He held a sign with my name on it. I had expected Dr.

Krabbendam (Dr. K), the ministry director, to meet me, but instead this Ugandan ushered me into a fourteen-passenger taxi van and assured me that Dr. K was waiting for me at the Nairerembe Guest House in Kampala. Though we were the only passengers, the driver started the van and headed to the house.

I learned that Moses was my driver and Rashid, who was a happy, friendly man with a huge smile, was my escort. He told me he had been a Muslim in a large polygamous family (this was a new concept to me), but Dr. K found him and shared the gospel with him. Rashid gave his life to Christ and began working for the Africa Christian Training Institute in Uganda as their Administrative Coordinator. To this day he is working with Dr. K.

When we arrived, we joined other short-term teams who had gathered at the guesthouse – all were going from there to different places. I was the only one without a team; I was traveling alone, though I was confident the Lord was going with me. I had no idea how He would use me, but I came with an open heart and mind. I came with a willingness to be used. My journey into the heart of Africa had begun – the journey the Lord had planned for me and prepared me for, even before I was born.

This new adventure in my life turned out to be life changing. I was not sure what the Lord would have me doing, but I was excited to be in the country where He had put my heart so many years before. Looking back, I realize the truth of the Scripture that the tragedies in my past were the troubles that provided the training for me to comfort others in my future:

> *Praise be to the God and Father of our Lord Jesus Christ, the Father of compassion and the God of all comfort, who comforts us in all our troubles, so that we can comfort those in any trouble with the comfort we ourselves have received from God. For*

just as the sufferings of Christ flow over into our
lives, so also through Christ our comfort overflows
(2 Corinthians 1:3-5).

My training started many years ago. I was the only girl out of five children, which caused me to be a bit spoiled and at times a bit lonely, but even then I had a heart for the broken, downtrodden, and injured. Any stray animal that needed help came home with me, and I bandaged, fed, and loved those helpless creatures. When I brought a little bird with a broken wing home, my mother warned me, "You are too kind. People will take advantage of you." I didn't understand; I only knew they needed care.

Caring for the animals relieved me for a short while from the loneliness I experienced in school. I had buckteeth and wasn't pretty. Frankly, I was a nerd, so my classmates teased me and made fun of me. Because of my teeth, the boys called me "buck duck." I felt so ugly I'd go home at night and cry, alone in my room. This made me wonder what on earth I was here for. Why was I existing in what seemed like such a cold world?

My one friend, Brian, lived in my neighborhood and went to my school. He was kind of a nerd too, but he said he loved Jesus, belonged to Him, and was going to heaven when he died. Brian was always happy no matter what was going on or who was teasing him, and I admired that. I asked him questions about Jesus, but I did not understand his answers. Sometimes I would go home and ask my mom about all this, and she would try to help me understand.

One day, when two small children wandered into a busy street, Brian jumped up, ran into the street, and shoved those children out of the way of oncoming traffic. He saved the children, but the car hit him, and he died. Brian, my only friend, was dead.

I was upset and lonely. Brian had been such a good friend to play with. Who would I ride bikes with now? Who would talk to me about the problems we had in the third grade?

Then everyone at school talked about Brian being a hero, and I became angry, because they had teased him when he was alive and treated him badly. Why would they say such nice things now? All of this made me wonder even more why we were here, but Brian had found purpose and loved the Lord. When he gave his life for those children, he touched my heart and life also. My training had begun, and unknown to me, seeds were planted.

Chapter Two

From Ridiculed to Redeemed

If you confess with your mouth, "Jesus is Lord," and believe in your heart that God raised him from the dead, you will be saved. Romans 10:9

When I became a teenager, the dentist fit me with braces to reposition my protruding teeth. This barb wire fence in my mouth only added physical pain to the cold, cruel world of my classmates who continued to mock, pester, and tease me – especially the boys. They changed my name from "buck duck" to "tinsel teeth." I continued to come home from school, sit down on the floor near my bed, and cry. What on earth was I here for? Why did God make me like this? I wondered why I even existed. I lacked the hope that those who know Jesus have, but that would eventually change.

My brother Dennis had ileitis, a rare disease of the small intestine, which caused the intestine to burst one night. He was rushed to the hospital, into surgery, and nearly died. While he was there, he wondered whether God was real. He did not have any more answers than I did, but he had a friend who did. This friend knew that God said, *you will seek me and find me when you seek me with all your heart,* so he shared the gospel with Dennis, and Dennis accepted Christ (Jeremiah 29:13).

After that, my dear brother spent a lot of time talking to me and sharing with me. He thought I wasn't listening, but I was. My life changed after my fourteenth birthday when my parents gave me a Bible, and being the curious person I was, I read about the burning bush and Moses. I had always thought Moses was just a man in the movies – you know, Charlton Heston in the *The Ten Commandments.* I learned that Moses was a real man who was raised by Pharaoh's daughter and later delivered his people from the Egyptians. Unbeknownst to me, it was all true.

I also discovered that "David and Goliath" was not just a kid's story that people liked to dramatize. David was a real man who heard the taunting and teasing of Goliath, ran toward the Philistine army, and flung the stone that hit the giant in the forehead. David's strong faith touched me, for I knew the stone had not really killed Goliath, but God had. I asked God to give me faith like David's and a heart for Him too.

I asked my mom and dad many questions about the Bible and watched religious programs on television because I wanted to know more. I especially liked the Billy Graham crusades. One evening when I was almost fifteen, I watched one of his crusades; his message was so clear: *For all have sinned and come short of the glory of God* and *The wages of sin is death, but the gift of God is eternal life in Christ Jesus our Lord* (Romans 3:23; 6:23). I cried, bowed my head, and asked the Lord to forgive me for my sins. I accepted Jesus Christ as my Savior. I realized that He died for me, and He was raised from the dead. He loved me so much that He was seeking me. I cried – not only because I was sorry for my sins but also because I discovered that someone could love me so much that He would die for me.

I could relate to Jesus because He lived a simple life, moving around and loving people. He helped them and told them nothing but truth. He always did what He knew the Father in heaven wanted Him to do, and after the people killed Him, He still loved them. I found this hard to understand, and it touched my heart and soul. People wanted Jesus crucified, and they mocked Him. Yet, He continued to love them and died for them anyway. This Man did not have a place to call home, or a job, or children, or a wife. He was a simple, humble Man who loved us.

After this, I told my parents that we needed to go to church, and they agreed. They had been thinking about it when they started buying Bibles for everyone's birthday. It was the year of the birthday Bibles. The first time I went to church with my parents and brothers was an eye opener for me; I enjoyed it but realized I had missed out on a lot for many years. The Sunday school surprised me with the good teaching, and I loved the music. Many people there were so friendly and accepting, I was completely amazed.

After we attended for about eight weeks, we were all baptized in front of the church. I had read about this in the Bible, and it fascinated me. Within a year I started teaching small children in Sunday school (four- and five-year-olds).

Jesus and the Bible captivated me so much that when I gave speeches at school, I spoke about Christian things and the gospel. My classmates were not surprised. After all, I was a nerd, so some of them laughed, but others listened without interruption, and a few became friends when they learned I was a Christian. However, my teacher did not appreciate my spiritual speeches, so she spoke to my dad about them and told him I should try speaking on other topics, but this did not stop me from talking about Jesus. My dad did not tell me to stop talking about Jesus either; he just shared what the teacher had said to him. He was glad that I was on fire for the Lord.

I would venture to say from all of this that I found out at the age of fifteen that I had the spiritual gift of evangelism. One of my classmates, Linda, accepted Christ as her Savior too, and we grew closer as friends.

Idi Amin

I also enjoyed reading *Life* magazine with its abundance of pictures and a variety of stories. You know, nerds watch news on TV and read news magazines. I learned about Idi Amin because many newspapers and magazines published articles about him, and television shows carried reports about him. He had taken over as dictator in Uganda in 1971 and lived a lavish lifestyle, while his printing of money and expulsion of Asians caused the economy to collapse around him.

Many questioned Amin's sanity, calling him mentally unstable, a madman, or buffoon. Rumors circulated that he had untreated syphilis that caused him to become the "Butcher of Uganda." Magazine articles reported that he even killed his older son, whom he loved, and ate his heart, because the witch doctor told him he would keep his son with him forever by doing that.

Statistics indicate that he killed 300,000 people – not only farmers, students, clerks, and shopkeepers but also cabinet ministers, Supreme Court judges, diplomats, the educated, and executives. His death squads, known as the Public Safety Unit, carried out most of the torture and killing.

As dictator of Uganda, Amin targeted and killed Christians and Hindus, leaving 800,000 orphaned children with no one to care for them. I loved children and babysat for many, so I prayed for those children in Uganda, children who needed to hear of the glorious grace of God. Soon I felt that God was telling me He wanted me to go there, so I wrote a letter about my desire to my grandmother and enclosed a poem – the poem that is at the beginning of this book. She saved that letter until I finally made it to Uganda.

Chapter Three

Troubles and Trials

For our light and momentary troubles are achieving
for us an eternal glory that far outweighs them all.
2 Corinthians 4:17

At last, in 1975 I had graduated from high school and was attending Joliet Junior College, where my dad was Dean of Administration. Unlike high school, I was popular and well liked in college. I had a job and a boyfriend – John. He had won the state wrestling championship for varsity his senior year of high school. We did not know each other then, but met later in college. We went to school parties and dances together. We'd hang out with our friends, and I'd go to his wrestling matches. We even went to the movies and an occasional dinner. The bewildering puzzle pieces of my life seemed to be fitting together to produce a normal-looking picture. In fact, my fairy tale was finally unfolding as Christmas approached with lights, music, laughter, and the love of my life.

But God tells us: *You do not even know what will happen tomorrow. What is your life? You are a mist that appears for a little while and then vanishes* (James 4:14). One day during that exciting time of my life, John headed out of town toward Macomb, Illinois, to pick up a friend at Western Illinois University to bring him home for Christmas. He reached over to tune the radio and swerved on the highway. He lost control, slipped off the pavement, and flipped over and over, shattering the windows and crushing the frame before reaching the bottom of the hillside and stopping. The driver's side smashed into his chest and punctured his lung. John died on the way to the hospital from internal bleeding. His best friend was in the car with him, but he had only minor cuts and bruises.

I went to John's funeral, and his mom and dad met me and walked me to the casket. I looked at him and became distraught; he was all wrong; his hands were wrong; his appearance wasn't right. They explained that one hand had been smashed, and the mortician did the best he could to put it back together and make it look "natural." Natural? How does a dead body look natural?

They invited me back to their home, because they wanted to give me some of their pictures. I saw all his things, but I was in such a daze that everything looked different from what I remembered – strange and surreal. I couldn't believe he was dead, but he was. I had lost a part of me, and the emptiness I knew in the past returned. The floodgates of my eyes opened again, and I had to wonder – was he the one for me? Why would God take him so quickly? I wondered if I would ever meet anyone I would be able to let myself love again.

About nine months after Christmas, Mom and Dad decided to move to Belleville, Illinois, to be closer to their parents who were elderly. Our house was for sale, and Dad had accepted a position as Vice President of Belleville Area College (now South Western Illinois College) and had already begun his new venture there during the fall semester. It would be a new beginning for all of us. However, I didn't want to go. All of my friends and life were in Joliet, and I wanted to stay there. My parents considered letting me stay, since I was working and could live with a good friend of mine.

Then one evening I had the dream, and I woke up feeling it was real. In my dream, someone kept telling me, "Mom is dead, she is really gone." That morning a friend had dropped my brother off for a visit; he lived in an apartment about four miles away. Mom said she would drive him back home. When I awoke, I realized my mom had already left to take him back. I tried to stop them, but they were halfway down the road. It was too late. I had a dreaded feeling that it was the last time I would see her as she was. It was just a dream. Even so, I was scared, as it seemed to be a warning from God.

I heard the sirens for a long time and wondered what was happening. When the phone rang, I was getting ready to wash my hair, and I dropped the bottle of green Prell Shampoo I was holding. It shattered into gooey glass shards all over the floor. A policeman calling from the hospital drove the dread into my heart. Mom had hit a pothole only a few miles from home and lost control of the car; they needed a family member's signature to take her to surgery. Even though they wanted someone older, I was the only one around, so they accepted me.

I called a friend to rush me to the hospital and left my younger brother, Gary, to take calls at the house. He did not want to stay but understood that he had to. After I signed the papers for surgery, they let me see her while they continued to clean blood from her many cuts. The broken glass of this morning and the broken glass that cut my mom, who looked fragile and broken, seemed to symbolize the brokenness in my life.

Mom was conscious as she took my hand and asked for Dad, and I assured her he was on the way. By that time everyone was on the way, but Belleville was a six-hour drive from the hospital. The doctors had to remove her spleen and three-fourths of her liver, but seven crushed ribs were poking her lungs, and a stomach ulcer started bleeding as a result of the surgical procedures. She had the equivalent of all her blood replaced with transfusions. She survived many surgeries and started the roller coaster ride of recovery. One day she'd be looking better, but the next she'd take a turn for the worse. Pastor Coop from Larken Baptist Church came almost every day to visit and pray, but when a fragile body is shattered, it cannot be easily put back together. After forty days, on October 26, 1976, my mother died.

We packed our belongings in Joliet as quickly as we could, but the day was a blur to me. I wanted to be strong for my brother and dad, but the tears in my eyes didn't cooperate. Weeping was not wrong, for God's Word tells us, *Blessed are you who weep now, for you will laugh,* so I wept (Luke 6:21). Neighbors brought food and some helped pack. My good friend, Karen, who had lost her father a few years before, also came and prayed with us.

When we had enough packed, we left for Missouri, where we buried my mom. The movers handled the rest of the household items, and we never went back. I lost my mother and left my friends at the same time, and my father did not want me to ever visit Joliet again. He wanted me home. However, I went back a few times, but that was all. At this point I could see that my dad and my younger brother needed me to be there for them, because the others were in the university or working.

Chapter Four

Even More Brokenness

The Lord is close to the brokenhearted and saves those who are crushed in spirit. Psalm 34:18

Having closed the Joliet chapter of our lives, I finished my studies in secretarial science, business, and bookkeeping and landed a job in a bank in Fairview Heights, Illinois. Beginning as a teller, I moved up to an assistant comptroller within a year, accepting the responsibilities of submitting federal reserve reports, overseeing teller balances, and reporting money coming in and going out. However, in my personal life, I was struggling to cope in a new town while missing my friends in Joliet.

We did not attend church regularly as a family, and I did not have a car to go on my own, so I watched religious programs on television again. I knew I needed a church and Christian friends, but felt incapable of finding them.

During this time, I tried to encourage my dad and brothers, reminding them that God is faithful, but they continued to struggle with the loss of Mom. However, 2 Timothy 2:13

reminds us that even *if we are faithless, he will remain faithful, for he cannot disown himself.* Nine months later, my dad met Margie and they were married within three months. I was not happy about him marrying so soon after Mom's death because I didn't really know Margie. The whole situation stressed me out, and I went from being the Maid of Honor at their wedding to rushing to the doctor with a bleeding ulcer. They gave me medicine and sent me home – alone. My grandmother from my dad's side came to stay with us for a few days, because she knew I was not feeling well.

I soon moved to St. Louis to live with my brother Ron who had finished his degree and worked as a police officer in St. Louis County. We made okay roommates since we were accustomed to each other, and I reconnected with Scott, a guy I had dated my senior year in high school – before John. He was going to school in St. Louis when we started dating again, and by this time, he was a Christian, so we got along well.

When school was out, Scott went home to visit his mother who was a widow. He took a part time job in construction, painting signs on roadsides. One day he fell off the ten-foot-high sign and broke his neck. He died instantly. I received the phone call at around 11:00 p.m. from his mom that he was dead. The pain I felt is hard to explain, but it was even worse that I couldn't take off work to go to the funeral. The tragedy was unbelievable to me, but the additional brokenness and hope-lessness were very real. Now I was becoming angry with God – my childhood friend had been killed; John had been killed; my mother was dead and my father remarried; and now, Scott had died too. What was the meaning of a life like this? I kept asking God, why? I could not find the answers.

At this time, I was working with Ernst & Ernst (now Ernst & Young), one of the largest accounting firms in the world. After two years of working there as a payable clerk and learning a little about doing budgets, I went to work for Coopers & Lybrand (now PricewaterhouseCoopers – the largest professional services firm in the world). Coopers & Lybrand heard about me from one of my friends who worked there; I was not looking for another job. The partner-in-charge at Ernst did not want me to leave and was not happy that I had gone to one of their rivals. I enjoyed my work at Coopers & Lybrand more, and the company soon offered to move me to Denver, Colorado, for a promotion. I only worked two years in the St. Louis office.

At twenty-four years old, I left everything behind for the second time and moved forward to Colorado, succeeding in business and excelling in administrative and financial responsibilities, but I was a failure on the inside, depressed and somewhat angry. I was falling into a deep pit. Putting all of my energy into work, my schedule at Coopers was regularly from 6:00 a.m. to midnight. With no time left for God, I strayed from Him. Instead of finding a good church, I hung out at bars and drank too much. Bennigan's Grill & Tavern was my favorite hangout, because I found friends who were down on their luck and needed to belong. Our late-night club had its own *Cheers* bar in the Mile-High city of Denver where we drowned our sorrows together and sometimes even cried together.

The *Cheers* bar atmosphere, however, did not bring inner peace, and I found myself wondering again what in the world I was doing here. Something kept tugging at me to change, to look elsewhere for the answers. Though I had strayed far from Jesus, I knew Him as my Savior and that kept me going even in my unhappiness, but life was losing the meaning I had in my early Christian years.

Some nights I would get in the car at Bennigan's and drive to 6th Avenue, a curvy highway in the mountains. I would speed around those curves and think about driving off the edge of cliffs and ending it all. Something always protected me from myself.

Sometimes I would stop by the side where the rapid river ran along the side of the highway, park my car in the trees to not be seen, and sit by the edge of the water and cry and scream at God. The cries and screams would turn into talking or prayers. I would say things like, "I thought you loved me God, why has there been so much heartache in my life? I want a normal life."

Then I met Phil when I was twenty-six years old. I thought this relationship might last, but it was not to be. Phil was funny and sweet, and I enjoyed talking with him. Sometimes we would laugh and have dinner together and talk about our dreams for the future. He said he was going to become a rich man and adopt a lot of children. Wow, this was a man after my own heart! One afternoon when he took me home from a date, we sat and looked at old photo albums. When we came across a picture of John and me with a news article about his accident, Phil asked me about him, so I told him about the tragedy and mentioned his name was John Phillip Santos. Phil laughed and said it was ironic because "my name is Phillip John." I asked him what was funny or ironic about that, and he just shrugged it off.

We went out for dinner that night, and Phil shared with me that he had some problems. This did not surprise me, because he hung out at Bennigan's with the rest of the down-and-outers. He did not seem to be like the others that hung out there; he seemed more successful – like he had it together. I asked him if he knew Jesus, and he said, "no." He also indicated that he was not even sure he believed in God. We talked more about it, but he had little more to say. I honestly felt that I could not be much of a witness to him since I hung out in a bar. This did make me think about my lifestyle.

The next morning when I went to my car to go to work, I found a note written in the dust on the frame, "I love you. Goodbye, Phil." A short time later I learned that he had gone home, sat in his car with the doors closed, engine running, and breathed in the exhaust until he fell asleep. He had killed himself.

News of his death made me go numb, and the tears began again until there were no more to come. As *David and his men wept aloud until they had no strength left to weep*, I had no more strength to cry (1 Samuel 30:4). Unlike David, who rescued their loved ones, I could not bring Phil back. I was angry and his friend Steve was angry too. We believed Phil did us an injustice by killing himself and leaving us. This time I felt more anger with Phil than I did with God, because I knew God did not tell him to kill himself. Steve told me Phil had been involved in cocaine and was in deep financial trouble because of it. I had no idea that Phil was involved in drugs, especially a drug like cocaine. I hated drugs because I saw how they destroyed my oldest brother's life. Phil never told me about this, so I had to find out from Steve after we buried him.

Then I wondered what would happen to him, for as far as I knew, he would go to hell because he did not know Jesus. I grieved as I blamed myself for not reaching out more but reminded myself that I didn't know everything that was going on in his life. I agonized in real pain, the pain of thinking someone I cared about went to hell, the pain of wondering if I could have done something to prevent it. This pain, instead of sending me back to the Lord, drove me further away, and I floundered more than ever to find meaning in life.

After this, I met Tim, who was a few years older than I was. I fell in love with him and thought we would marry. We met when I was twenty-eight years old at a New Year's Eve party. He asked me to dance and proceeded to tell me he was heartbroken and swearing off women for the New Year. I asked him why he wanted to dance then. We got along in a fun way from the beginning. Maybe my life would take a turn for the better. But he turned out to be a heavy drinker, not just a social drinker. He seemed to be an alcoholic like his father and older brother. We dated seriously for a year, but he seemed to just be playing games with me (though I've learned since, that was not so), and we were not good for each other. Tim showed up late at my home one night, a bit drunk, and told me about another woman he'd been seeing.

I was brokenhearted, if possible more than ever before. I was so broken, but the anger was gone, only the hurt remained. I knew I had left God out of my decisions, and something had to change. I knew I had thrown myself into some of the pits I got into. In the midst of my deep pain, I knew the Lord was there for me, *because I know whom I have believed, and am convinced that he is able to guard what I have entrusted to him for that day* (2 Timothy 1:12). I did have hope and went back to Jesus, realizing what He wanted in my life – not just to save me from my sins and hell but to have a relationship with me now.

I finally understood He loved me and wanted me to serve and love Him. I understood His forgiveness and that He wanted me to forgive too. I had a lot of forgiving and healing to do, but I was finally headed in the right direction. I was on my way back to the Lord.

Chapter Five

Short-term Mission Trips

And I said, "Here am I. Send me!" Isaiah 6:8

I had always loved children and enjoyed volunteering, so I joined Big Sisters and did things with my "little sister" in my spare time. When my first little sister moved away from the area, Maria was assigned to me. One day in July 1987, I suggested going to a Billy Graham crusade, and Maria agreed. The message was clear, as always, and even though Maria did not understand everything, she wanted to go forward. I went with her, and in the midst of all of those people, the tears began to fall, and I found myself crying and rededicating my life to Him. I understood afresh that He wants to be more than my Savior – He wants to be my Lord. He wants me to walk with Him every moment. His desire is for a relationship with me in a personal way, incorporating my heart, my love, all of me with no excuses, no frills, and no holding back.

I learned the lesson of Romans 8:38-39: *For I am convinced that neither death nor life, neither angels nor demons, neither the present nor the future, nor any powers, neither height nor depth, nor anything else in all creation, will be able to separate us from the love of God that is in Christ Jesus our Lord.* He does not leave us or forsake us, though we often do our own thing. He is still there waiting for us to talk to Him, love Him, and have a relationship with Him. He was there – waiting for me to come back to Him. His love never dies, and He is our strong tower during the rough times. The Psalmist tells us, *For you have been my refuge, a strong tower against the foe* (Psalm 61:3).

After that crusade, I found a church – Bear Valley Church in Lakewood – where I grew in my spiritual walk. They encouraged me and discipled me, and as I learned to look beyond myself, the yearning for missions was rekindled in my heart, and thoughts of Africa returned. My initial response to these foreign African thoughts was – no way! I hate bugs. I hate dirt. But God knew before I was born what He had planned for me. *For I know the plans I have for you, declares the Lord, plans to prosper you and not to harm you, plans to give you hope and a future* (Jeremiah 29:11). In the recesses of my heart and mind, I knew He had those plans.

Mexico City

In the meantime, however, God used my home church to prepare me for my life work. I became a member of the church and started attending the single's career group. Everyone in this group seemed to be interested in missions and a closer walk with the Lord. I joined a team of friends from Bear Valley Church and went to Mexico City in 1989 for two and a half weeks to teach and share the gospel. I taught four- and five-year-olds under a tree during a vacation Bible school at a brand new church. How I loved it! The children were sweet, excited, and full of questions. I only wished I knew the language better.

One day, as we sat under the tree, something dripped on one of the children. We all looked up into the tree and saw a dead dog that had been skinned. Sticky! Yuck! Disgusting and nauseating, this kind of evil was horrifying, but the people told us it was the work of Satan worshippers. They explained that many worship Satan and did repulsive and wretched things. I experienced anger of a different sort – foreboding and trepidation, but the Lord calmed me and made me want to share the gospel with them. What a thrill it was when people came to the Lord!

Once when we were praying in church, I spoke in Spanish even though I knew very little of the language. The message was for the church, and someone interpreted it for me, because I believe I was speaking in tongues. That was the only time it ever happened, but God must have had a specific message for that church. Apparently, it was encouraging to the people of the church.

While in Mexico City, I became friends with Martha, a fifteen-year-old girl who had suffered from many troubles and did not have a good family. Her father drank and often abused her mother; Martha's brother was not kind to her either. I shared the gospel with her, and we spent much time in prayer together. I told her that I needed to know the Bible better, and we all need to study God's Word. Martha grew in the Lord, and we have kept in touch through the years.

Martha and I reunited in 1990 when I traveled to Mexico on a vacation with my good friend Cindy. We paid for her transportation to come and visit us at the beach on the Pacific side, and she enjoyed being with us during that time. She had grown in the Lord, and we were excited to see that she was living for Him and having a genuine relationship with Jesus. By this time, she was in college, working, and felt God was blessing her, because her life was much better than before.

Urbana Missions Conference

In 1990 I went to the Urbana Missions Conference that is held every three years in Urbana, Illinois. Thousands of people (mostly young) from around the world come to receive special teaching from some of the missionaries around the world. A lady named Karen touched me in a special way. She talked about being in South America for twenty-five years and how the Lord was using her, though the hardest thing for her was to die to self. Dying to self was a new concept to me, and I asked her questions. We prayed together, and she gave me a deeper understanding of what "I surrender all" really means.

I met Joni Erickson Tada, and we discussed missions. She was one of the teachers and represented a mission that worked with the handicapped. She asked me what I was waiting for, why had I not gone, but I couldn't answer. In spite of being paralyzed from a diving accident, she is a good teacher, writer, and wonderful encourager in the Lord. God has blessed her so much, and she suffered much more than I ever did. The joy of the Lord shines in her, and it reached out to me. I realized how good my life had been compared to hers, yet she was very happy. In many ways, in spite of the accident, she had been blessed.

I began reading books like *Candles in the Dark* by Amy Carmichael, the missionary to India, and books by George Mueller, the man of prayer. They became my heroes, but Jesus is and always will be my greatest hero.

I also met Steve Green, the main singer at the conference – and what a man of God he is! The theme song at the conference was "May All Who Come Behind Me Find Me Faithful," but my favorite song became "The Mission." If you can imagine about 20,000 people, all interested in missions in different parts of the world, together singing with Steve Green, "To love the Lord our God is the heartbeat of our mission . . ." – what a thrill this was and a blessing.

My most significant moment, however, was when a young man named Simon from The Africa Christian Training Institute introduced me to Dr. Henry Krabbendam (Dr. K), who stood six feet three inches tall and spoke with a slight German accent. Dr. K said that he would help me go to Africa, so I was to notify him when I was ready. He sent me the papers and information on the culture and dress, money I had to raise, where that money goes, and what I had to do. He also asked me to write a letter explaining what I wanted to do. I wrote and told him I wanted to build an orphanage and help about two hundred children and teach everyone I meet about Jesus and what He has done for them.

Costa Rica

The very next year, I went to Costa Rica with Cherry Creek Presbyterian Church in Denver on a church planting trip. I only knew the two pastors, one from Costa Rica, who were leading the team.

Oh, the spiders. Many, many spiders, and I hate spiders – creepy, crawly spiders and scooting, scurrying spiders. Other than that, the country was beautiful. We learned much by talking to people and living in a different culture for two weeks, but it takes years to grasp a thorough understanding.

I struggled in Costa Rica, because the other girls were not friendly at first. Most of them came from rich families and were younger than me. I made an effort to spend time with them, but they didn't seem to be into praying. That disturbed me, but things changed when we went into the inner city of San Juan to work on the church building. First, we tore down the old building, and then we began the foundation of the new building, which other teams would finish at a later date.

That evening while still in the inner city, we hung a white sheet up and showed the movie *The Cross and the Switchblade*, an old Christian film about Nicky Cruz, a teen gang member whose life was transformed by David Wilkerson's ministry. A Costa Rican gang was at the movie and was not happy about it, so they threw stones at us and said terrible things. We took off running and hid. I helped the other girls find a safe place and then maneuver away from the gang. They told me they were thankful I was there, and I told them I was just trusting God. I could see they were all scared. I did not usually feel fear, because I really did trust in the Lord for protection, especially when I was serving Him. I have always known that when it is my time to die, it is in God's hands and not mine or anyone else's.

During my time in Costa Rica, I became friends with the wonderful lady who kept me in her home, even though hers had been a hard life. She had two children about my age, and when I was sick, she treated me like one of her own. She was living the gospel: *For I was hungry and you gave me something to eat, I was thirsty and you gave me something to drink, I was a stranger and you invited me in, I needed clothes and you clothed me, I was sick and you looked after me* (Matthew 25:35-36). After her husband died, life had become harder for her. They lived with bars on the windows and a wall around their home to keep safe, but she shared that the Lord was taking care of her.

New York

In 1992 I left Coopers & Lybrand to go back to school while I worked with an organization called The Resolution Trust Corporation on a contract for the federal government on the failed Savings & Loan project. God blessed me by providing all fees for my schooling. I finished a degree in Human Resources at Colorado Christian University (CCU), where I wrote a personnel manual as a thesis for The Denver Rescue Mission and received credit for a year of study in the Bible, which was required for graduation.

I attended every mission conference and seminar I could and even ran into Joni Erickson Tada again at a women's conference in Denver. She asked me the same question again, what are you still doing here? Again, I could not answer her, but she told me if she sees me again, she had better hear that I finally went.

That year I had the opportunity to go to the inner city of Brooklyn in New York twice. The first time I went with a team of friends, and we worked with many different ministries in various parts of the ghettos. One individual, Bill Wilson with Mission to America, touched my heart. He worked with 10,000 kids every Saturday – kids who were bused in from all areas of New York. I enjoyed what he was doing with his Saturday Sunday school. He offered me a position on his staff doing the accounting work, but I feared it would delay what I knew the Lord was calling me to do. Now he is busing about 20,000 children into Sunday school on Saturdays from different ghettos in New York. What an amazing ministry and how the Lord is using him and the staff there.

During these mission trips, I realized how little I knew about the Bible, even though I had been reading it every day. I didn't have Scripture memorized like some of the others on the teams, and I felt inadequate. I learned not only that I should hide God's Word in my heart, but the Psalmist also tells us that *the unfolding of your words gives light; it gives understanding to the simple* (Psalm 119:130). I recognized the need for hope and love in people's lives, knowing the only thing that can fill our hearts completely is Jesus Christ. I poured myself into the Scriptures and took courses with The Denver Seminar like *How to Share Your Faith Without an Argument*. I worked in the inner city of Denver whenever I had the chance and shared the gospel with teenagers, prostitutes, and homeless, working together with Mile High Ministries through Bear Valley Church.

Then in 1993, Dr. K called and asked if I was coming to

Uganda that year, but the dust was still settling from Desert Storm, so I said, "not this year." Finally, in 1994, I said, "*Here am I.*" I went for three weeks – and that was how I found myself at the Guest House in Kampala about to be whisked away to the heart of Africa, alone, alone with the Lord.

Chapter Six

Plunging into Poverty

If there is a poor man among your brothers in any of the towns of the land that the Lord your God is giving you, do not be hardhearted or tightfisted toward your poor brother. Rather be openhanded and freely lend him whatever he needs. Deuteronomy 15:7-8

That first trip to Uganda was a whirlwind of activity. After I arrived in Entebbe at 6:30 a.m. and had my encounter with the AK-47-carrying guard, I was rushed off to the Guest House in Kampala where Dr. K held an orientation and served us a breakfast of the most wonderful pineapple. He was clearly in charge, sending teams in different directions while at the same time making me feel at ease. He explained where I'd be going and with whom I'd be staying. Then he introduced me to Olive and Harriet, sisters belonging to the first family I'd stay with. By 10:30 a.m. I was on an express bus that was headed to the village of Kamonkoli.

"Express" didn't accurately describe the bus. We didn't leave Kampala until it was full, which was about noon. The word *full* gained new meaning to me as a goat, several chickens, and people stood over me, radiating odors throughout the area. I kept telling myself not to be weak and get sick. This was a different world, and I had to adapt fast. The people were friendly, however, and I wondered how they could stand so long. Not even the cockroaches crawling on the floor of the bus or the chickens with biting mites seemed to disturb them. I did not take to the creepy crawling insects or the chickens pecking at my feet and was quite uncomfortable. However, I became more uncomfortable when one of the goats decided to make a mess on the floor of the bus – and it smelled! Only excitement and the knowledge that I could be used by God kept me going.

The road was only paved part of the way, and I had to fight to stay in my seat as we bumped along. The dust rolled in through the open windows, but the heat prevented us from closing them. The chickens and goats kept "dropping their stuff" all over the bus, and the smell nearly caused me to vomit.

In contrast to the crowded chaos inside the bus, I was shocked at the beauty beyond the windows – a contradiction of environments. Rows and rows of tea bushes lined the plantations in luscious green scenery. Sugar cane fields followed the tea plantations, and then we passed a forest area that had many big trees. I managed to see a few monkeys in what I later found out was the Mabira Forest.

I also caught glimpses of Lake Victoria, which I knew nothing about at the time. I later looked it up on a map and found it to be the second largest great lake in the world – second only to Lake Superior.

It was 8:00 p.m. when, smeared with dust, we reached Mbale town. Standing up was a great relief since I had just arrived on an airplane that morning at 6:30 a.m. before my all-day bus ride. I was famished and thirsty and needed to use the bathroom in a bad way. We were greeted by wonderful, loving, warm people who did not mind waiting there for me, ready to cater to whatever I wanted. Since I was hungry, they asked what I'd like to eat. I said, "A hamburger," and then laughed, never expecting to get one. Within thirty minutes, they brought me a hamburger. I was surprised to say the least. It tasted very good, and I enjoyed it with the chips they brought.

The bathroom was another story. The words *bath* and *room* do not rightfully describe the pit latrine – a hole in the ground that you squatted over. I held my skirt high to avoid the liquid all around the hole and chose not to think about it. The flies, cockroaches, and spiders did a good job of distracting me from the wet hole, and the darkness helped as well. I was being baptized into the culture.

I had assumed this was our destination but learned that this was only the end of the line for taxis and buses. To reach the village of Kamonkoli, we traveled by another means – some kind of car. It was 10:00 p.m. and raining when we arrived, exhausted and dirty, but the family that welcomed me was the friendliest and warmest family I had ever encountered. I was already falling in love with the people and Uganda. Not only were they friendly and warm, they had prepared a huge dinner and waited to eat until after we sang and prayed. This family had so many people that I could not remember all the names.

When I awoke the next morning, the breathtaking beauty stunned me. The rays of the sun were peeking through, and I looked out on beautiful Wanale Mountain in front of the huge Mt. Elgon. Birds sang – but I was speechless. After eggs and bread with tea made in milk with lots of sugar, I met more of the family. They kept coming and coming, and I wondered where they all stayed, because the house was small. Margaret and Nimrod, the parents, had twelve children, which included a set of twins and a set of triplets.

We sang worship songs and prayed before going out into

the village. The poverty around me was worse than any I had ever seen, even worse than in Mexico. I wondered if anyone owned a pair of shoes. The people lived in the dirt, slept in the dirt, ate in the dirt, and even made their houses from sticks and mud with grass on top. No beds, no furniture, no stoves, no refrigerators, no bed covers or curtains. Rags for clothes. They cooked with firewood that they gathered and used three stones to hold a pan over the fire. Many children had big bellies and puffy cheeks, and I knew that this was from worms, which could cause malnutrition. No pictures I had ever seen on television or in magazines had depicted the gravity of the poverty.

Cooking without a kitchen

The poverty was not just in material goods but also in spiritual health. People needed the love of Christ in their hearts. What would that look like to them? How could I handle this without my emotions going completely out of control? What would Jesus do? These questions kept haunting me. No training in the world could prepare me for what I was up against here in this village in Uganda of East Africa. My eyes were opened but so was my heart, and I would have to depend on the Holy Spirit to know how to minister here.

Poverty

Families opened their homes to me, so I could talk with them and share from the Bible. I must have appeared like a strange alien, for the children gathered around and wanted to touch my hair and skin to see what it was like. Their eyes grew big as they were fascinated with the "muzungu" coming to their home. People came from other homes nearby and gathered to listen to what the "muzungu" had to say. I was excited to learn how hungry they were to hear the gospel, making me eager to share more and more.

I shared a room in an unfinished house with a bat. I slept in the bed at night, and he slept on the ceiling in the day. My bed was small but adequate, though I had no net to cover the whole bed. Thankfully, I had brought a small one from home that protected my head. No electricity, no running water, and all I had for light was an old kerosene lantern. The bathroom was a pit latrine outside, and we carried water to bathe in that *same* latrine. I didn't care though, because I was thankful to be serving the Lord where I believed He wanted me.

My focus was on Christ and what He wanted, not on myself. When we serve the Lord, we cannot get caught up in the things around us and lose focus. Jesus said we should keep our eyes fixed on Him and His kingdom. We must deny ourselves, which requires focus and the Spirit's leading.

I traveled on the back of a bicycle called a "boda boda," and sometimes I walked. Bicycles gained the name boda boda during Idi Amin's reign when people were running for the border. They would yell, "Boda boda," which was "border border" for short. The name stuck. These bicycles were the main form of transportation, and the bicyclists hurried everywhere on the road, carrying people wherever they needed to go. They were plain, old, rickety bicycles with a cushioned seat on the back for passengers. Some carried more than one passenger, but I refused because I was thrown off a few times when it was raining and ended up in the mud. Most of the time, however, we walked wherever we went. I didn't mind because I was used to exercise and in good shape. In fact, nothing seemed to bother me, because I was so happy to be here and share the love of Christ that nothing else mattered.

The children excited me the most – so many faces of young ones. One day we decided to help them with some physical problems like ring worm, jiggers in the feet, and bathing. I was surprised to learn that most of these children had never had a bath as we know it, so we taught them about bathing. Most of the people in the village did not even have an outhouse, so bathing was done in the trees with papyrus sticks or banana leaves sewed together for an element of privacy. Soap was for the rich people only. Toilets were the bushes nearby, but one never knew which bushes were in use, so we had to be careful where we stepped.

Jiggers were new to me. They are like ticks, and many of the children had them in their feet and toes. We had to dig them out because as they fed on blood, they got bigger and bigger. They hurt and they itch. Eventually, they would burst and release baby jiggers to continue the feeding frenzy. We dug them out with a sterilized needle, which hurt and the children were not happy about it. Of course, no one likes a person sticking them with needles. None of the children we worked with that particular day had ever worn shoes. Occasionally, one might have a pair of slippers, but only the rich had shoes.

Many of the children hung out in the mango trees. I asked about this and learned that often they go to school without breakfast, so they would climb a tree and get a mango to eat. They do not receive anything for lunch at school, so once again, they climb a tree and eat. Sometimes, if the parents or guardians are caring, they get a meal in the evening. Otherwise, they get a lot of vitamin C.

I met one twelve-year-old girl who had fallen from a mango tree. Her poor body was twisted and bent, and she could no longer walk or sit up. Her parents had no money, so they could do nothing to help her when this happened. She lay in the dirt and dragged herself with her arms. When I finally had enough funds, I was told it was too late, and they could do nothing for her. Medical capabilities were, and are still, very limited. Many children suffer their whole lives because of a lack of funds to get the medical help that is needed.

Often the parents or guardians did not seem to care about the children, as I remember my parents caring, and the cycle of neglect and abuse is vicious. Many parents grew up without love and, therefore, do not know how to love. I ached for these people and their need for Jesus. The children needed love, but so did the parents and guardians. Most had no hope and saw no reason to live or care, much like me in my own struggles. Only Jesus could mend their hearts and teach them differently.

For a week, we shared the gospel with the people and played with the children, seeing many give their lives to Christ. But it was time to leave whether I wanted to or not. I kept asking about follow-up with the people, but no answers were available. How would they ever find hope?

The Mango Tree

Chapter Seven

Ft. Portal

*Defend the cause of the weak and fatherless; main-
tain the right of the poor and oppressed.* Psalm 82:3

From Kamonkoli I went to the airport to fly to Ft. Portal in
an MAF plane (Mission Aviation Fellowship). This plane
was small and only held three passengers and little luggage. From
the air we viewed of the luscious tea fields with people moving
up and down the rows, picking the leaves. The sugar cane looked
like big stalks waving in the wind. The big mountains of the
Rwenzori Mountain Range that borders the Democratic Republic
of Congo and Uganda and part of Rwanda were breathtaking.

But as we flew over Lake Victoria and parts of Rwanda, we
saw dead bodies everywhere, as the genocide in Rwanda was
still going on at this time. What a fearful, horrible sight! What a
contradiction of surroundings – the beauty of the lake with the
horror of the killing. It is hard to imagine how people can do
this to one another and leave all kinds of body pieces floating
in the water – heads, arms, legs. The haunting horror of that
sight is still with me today. I was told that many people were

fishing the body parts out at the head of the Nile and burying them as fast as they could in Uganda, because cholera had become a great concern to everyone.

When we reached Ft. Portal, I wondered where we were going to land, and how, since it was thundering and lightning, and the little plane was being tossed to and fro. I prayed, believing God did not bring me to Uganda to die in a small plane. When the pilot said we were landing on a strip of cleared land, all I saw were trees and a patch of grass. I braced myself when I saw the small landing spot on top of a small mountain, but we made it. Bumpy and terrifying, yes, but I loved it all. Much better than a rollercoaster.

Our time in Ft. Portal was different from the work we did in Kamonkoli, and living conditions seemed to be a little better, but people were still poverty stricken. We, however, stayed in the guesthouse for World Harvest Missions, which was much more modern than the home in Kamonkoli. We even had an inside shower. No running water, but a shower space to stand in while we used the water from a basin with a cup. They had set up a water purifier for drinking water, which was easier than boiling water all the time.

We met other missionaries who were working in another village in the area that sounded very primitive and had a wonderful dinner with them at the Colonial Hotel restaurant, which was fancier than any I had seen in Uganda.

With a little bit of snow on top, the Rwenzori Mountains provided beautiful scenery. Some mountains were over 17,000 feet high, with the tallest one, Mountain of the Moon, at 17,200 feet.

Again the people were warm and friendly, easy to love. Olive and I went into schools and shared the gospel, giving our testimonies to students and teachers. After sharing Scripture with them, I told them about the man with a wheelbarrow:

"There was a man with a wheelbarrow who decided to go

across Victoria Falls on a tightrope. He asked the people if they thought he could make it. They cheered him on and said, 'Yes, we believe you can do it.' As he proceeded, the crowd grew and was excited to watch him.

"After he made it across and back once, he put a hundred pounds of dirt in the wheelbarrow and asked again, 'Do you think I can make it?' The people cheered again and he went over.

"When he got back, a man in the front yelled, 'I believe, I believe you could take anything across the falls and come back.'

"So the man with the wheelbarrow looked at him after cleaning the dirt out and said, 'Okay, then you're next.' The man took off running because he didn't really believe."

Then I related this to how the Lord wants us to trust and believe and get into the wheelbarrow, whatever that situation may be, and move to the other side where we will be with Him forever.

The students responded and wanted to ask the Lord to live in their hearts, and they wanted to live their lives for Christ. Again, I wondered about follow-up – who would do it? Several asked if we would come back and teach more and bring Bibles. They were living examples of Psalm 119:20, which says, *My soul is consumed with longing for your laws at all times.* I left all the information with the Anglican Church and the World Harvest Mission as well as the Presbyterian Church.

We visited a babies' home filled with infants who had been left with no one to care for them. They had been abandoned and then found, or the parents had died. Hundreds of babies were suffering in the area, and the home had been built with good intentions of caring for them. But, the care they were receiving was not good. The feeding was inadequate. The home smelled from urine and baby poop. Diapers, food, and everything else was in short supply. My heart broke for these dear babies, and I wanted to just take them home with me and give them a better life. I was so frustrated I cried that evening and talked to the Lord for a very long time, because at the end of the week, a small plane took us back to Entebbe and then to Kampala. Who would care for these children?

Chapter Eight

Kampala Slums

All they asked was that we should continue to remember the poor, the very thing I was eager to do.
Galatians 2:10

Here I worked in the worst slums I had ever seen – certainly worse than the New York City slums I'd seen. I worked the area, evangelizing with two men, Brian and Jim. Many of these people were not as friendly and warm as in Ft. Portal or Kamonkoli, and they seemed to be bitter about their lives. With a focus on money that disturbed me, they were a bit quarrelsome and sometimes angry. I had to keep asking myself how I would feel if I were in their shoes and without Christ. The city smelled from pollution, and garbage was thrown everywhere.

And why shouldn't they be bitter? Many of them had migrated from the north because of the war going on with the Lord's Resistance Army (LRA) and their leader, Joseph Kony, but their escape turned to despair, as Kampala could not absorb the flood of people. Hundreds of thousands ended up in these slums, as they sought to leave poverty and war but found hardship and disease. Stagnant water all over the area led to inadequate safe water and lack of sanitation, not to mention an increase in mosquitos.

Kampala Slums

These conditions continue even today. Most of these people are uneducated and have no skills, so decent employment is almost impossible to find. Some young men and women had tried to escape the LRA, and others came looking to find a better future but ended up in the slums when they couldn't find work. Without expertise in any field, they became desperate and turned to casual labor, petty businesses, commercial sex, illegal business, and crime. In desperation, they now abuse and sell drugs and buy and sell sex, increasing the rate of HIV/AIDS infections.

Poverty also drives women to the alcohol trade. They brew "malwa," an alcoholic drink brewed from millet, but these women work in unsanitary conditions along with food that they make for sale. Filthy drainage channels separate the shabby homes, making the water unsafe to wash in, much less consume.

These conditions cause the slums to be full of other diseases also – malaria, tuberculosis, and cholera run rampant. The HIV-infected individuals can't afford good food, and that makes them more susceptible to all of these diseases. Much ignorance and misinformation contribute to the inability to prevent such sicknesses.

Legal polygamy also adds to the spread of HIV, because the men have many wives and believe the more children they have, the more they look like real men. Teaching them that they are more of a man by being responsible is a difficult task, but I try to help them understand that God expects them to care for their wives and children. Even helping them accept legal marriages presents a problem, because they cannot afford the dowry of goats, cows, chickens, and food that must be paid to the parents or guardians of the women. So, polygamy flourishes, as does AIDS.

The people don't seem to care because they have no hope and little to live for. Getting AIDS and dying is just part of life. What else is there?

This deplorable situation gives rise to high levels of noise and increasing rates of crime. The cycle of poverty, crime, and disease goes around and around. Much of the solution lies with education, but the schools are not free and require uniforms, which the children cannot afford. Sponsorships seem to be the answer to increase literacy and teach skills needed to obtain better employment. Christ is the only answer to give them hope through salvation and a relationship with Him.

One thing I learned: Even though life is difficult in Uganda, the Spirit of the Lord was moving, so the hardships didn't bother me. We walked a lot and then we walked more. Outside of the slums, the markets were fun to visit, and I learned to bargain for pineapples, potatoes, and tomatoes. I was not fond of the meat, however, as the beef, goat, and other meat hung in the heat with flies all over it. Who knows how much dust collects on it?

In spite of these conditions, the Lord was growing a great love in me for these people whose lives were difficult beyond comprehension. What I saw was normal for them, for they had never known anything else. But somehow they still knew something was missing. I could not forget the heartbreaking hopelessness in the eyes of the children. Hope deferred produced eyes that begged to be loved, to be cared for, and to love in return.

Public school

Chapter Nine

Return to Uganda

Seek justice, encourage the oppressed. Defend the
cause of the fatherless, plead the case of the widow.
Isaiah 1:17

The three weeks in Uganda flew by, and when I returned to America, my heart yearned to be back. I wanted to return and serve the Lord in Uganda, amazed that God knows where He can use us and where we will be happy. He knew I would love the Ugandan people and children.

When sharing the gospel of Jesus Christ with them, I recovered the spiritual gift of evangelism, and several people accepted Christ during that time, but their longing eyes begged for more. They needed hope. They needed prayers and teaching from the Word of God.

I prayed for them; I prayed for me; I prayed for God to lead me. My heart and mind assured me that God wanted me back in Uganda, but how could I give up my job and life in Colorado? How could I pick up and move to Africa? How could I venture out alone? Which organization would I go with? How does it all work?

I wrote to Dr. K and told him what was on my heart. I wanted to build an orphanage for at least two hundred children, provide hope, and establish capable community members. Dr. K suggested I come back and see how God directed me.

When I first told my dad I was going back, he asked me if I had lost my mind. "Why would anyone give up a good paying job and nice home to live in Africa?" The rest of the family agreed with him, but I referred them to Luke 14:33 where the Lord tells his disciples they must count the cost of discipleship. Jesus said, "*any of you who does not give up everything he has cannot be my disciple.*"

They feared for my safety and did not want me to be so far away, but eventually they became accepting, supportive, and even excited about what God was doing through me and the ministry. However, it took some time for the Lord to get them to this point of believing that God wanted this in my life.

I proceeded to raise funds by visiting churches and people and sharing the vision that God had laid on my heart for the children in Uganda. Most were friendly and welcoming, but I received many "thank you, but no thanks." Finding people who shared the vision was hard, discouraging work. More people than just my family thought I was crazy. I was not discouraged however, as my heart had stayed in Uganda where God put it.

In June 1995, I gave notice at my job, sold everything I owned, and headed to Uganda. A new journey, bringing glory to God in Uganda, began as I stepped off the plane in Entebbe. A journey of a life dedicated to Christ and raising children for Him. But, now I needed direction. I was given a work permit and assigned to the Presbyterian Church for one year.

I investigated what others were doing in the area, because I needed to know how they were helping. I found some Bible

studies and church planters. One individual was translating
the Bible into one of the fifty-two tribal languages, and I met
another who was doing the same work God was leading me
to do. I had evangelized in the inner cities of Denver and New
York, but with little reception. No one really wanted to listen.
But here in Uganda, people were hungry for the gospel and
many accepted Christ. The living conditions seemed to make
the people desperate for help – desperate for hope.

One would think the situation would improve after Idi Amin
was forced out. However, because of the rapid spread of AIDS
and its devastating effects, the number of orphans had grown
to 1.5 to 2 million in Uganda alone.

I found many orphanages, but only one of them was in
operation. The missionaries had abandoned them and left the
facilities for nationals to run, hoping they were sustainable. But,
sometimes no funds were available or the nationals misused
those funds. This discouraged me, but I tried not to let it lead
me in a different direction. I filed the information in the back
of my mind and heart for future reference.

Members of the government claimed these orphans had
many more problems than before they came to the orphanages, because now they didn't know their extended families.
They had nowhere to go.

I determined not to be one of those who deserted the children.
I knew that if God called us to do something, He is faithful and
just to complete it. The apostle Paul tells us that he was *confident of this, that he who began a good work in you will carry it
on to completion until the day of Christ Jesus* (Philippians 1:6).

The people in Kamonkoli were preparing a small house
for me, but until it was ready, I stayed in the same house I had
been in before, which belonged to a man working for the government who was related to Christine, Harriet, and Olive. At
the time, the house was old and falling apart with a tin roof

that leaked. The room had no ceiling and the one window had no screen. But, I did have a decent bed, a simple wood frame with a high-density foam mattress, and a small table next to it.

Walking Kamonkoli

Once again I bathed in the outhouse in the back yard, which was the pit latrine. Using the outhouse as both toilet and bathing room made for a bad, smelly experience. To my horror, spiders occupied every corner of my outhouse, and cobwebs laced each corner and crack and attacked me in the face when I entered. I decided the time had come to clean this place up before another bath or short call.

While the spiders kept me company in the outhouse, a bat once again took up residence in my one-room house. He stayed up in the roof area, which was fine with me. But, at night, he liked to wake up and move around. Harriet came to stay with me for the first few weeks but then left for school. She was going to the university in Kenya and had a sponsor to help her. Olive also joined us, so the three of us slept in one small room. Harriet got scared at night, so we sometimes slept with the lantern on.

One night I asked her why she was so scared. She told me stories of her past and then stories of the witch doctors and the witchcraft that goes on. I wasn't sure I believed any of this was true at the time. I remember laughing and thinking she was just scared sometimes. It was funny, because she often scared herself when she told the stories.

I had no kitchen or running water, but I cooked on two small, smelly, kerosene camping stoves, called paraffin stoves. I thought of myself as a pioneer back in the early 1800s in the States, thinking it must have been like this. With my two saucepans and a few dishes, I cooked my rice, beans, and sometimes chicken and potatoes, but my preference was for fresh foods. Adjustments to this life were hard, and sometimes at night I'd go to my room, shut the door, and cry about things I had witnessed during the day. I was lonely too, but I didn't want to hinder the children's budding trust – their hope for hope.

I remember the first chicken someone gave me after sharing the Word of God in their home. I named it Freddy and kept it in a small storage area. On the day Harriet went to kill it, I was shocked and had to leave the house. Wow, I was going to eat Freddy! This was another new experience for me. Cleaning it after it was killed was hard, and I couldn't eat it later, though everyone else seemed to enjoy it.

I had little in the line of material possessions. I gave most of the money from the sale of my things and my personal bank account to Harriet's mother for the clinic – her dream and a big need in the village. With no other clinics around, she was operating out of a mud hut. She treated malaria, delivered babies, and dressed wounds with a minimum of supplies. I used the rest of my money for school fees for a few children, because none of the schools in Uganda were free, not even the government schools, and they often had more than two hundred children in a class, sitting on dirt floors. They had no books for studying, and even the teachers lacked real training.

My return brought excitement, but the dire conditions

often seemed overwhelming. So many needs, so few workers, so little money. But God had led me to this little village to do a work for Him. He would increase my faith in the days ahead, and together we would accomplish His work and bring glory to Him in Uganda.

Chapter Ten

One Small Child

Let the little children come to me, and do not hinder them, for the kingdom of heaven belongs to such as these. Matthew 19:14

After being in the country for two months, I was out with Christine, a sister to Olive and Harriet (who were at school), when we came to a home where I had been sharing the gospel. A little boy named David lived there at the time with his grandmother Mary. His parents didn't acknowledge him as their son because he had been born out of wedlock while they were still in high school. His job was to tend the cattle for his grandmother, even though he was only five.

David wore a little red tee shirt that was old and dirty and a pair of tan colored shorts that were tied on because they did not have elastic or a zipper. These were his only clothes. His hair was light in color, and he had the biggest brown sparkly eyes that melted my heart. I could not forget him. David looked somewhat sickly because he had a bad case of worms – what hope could a little one like that have? I went to the grandmother and asked her if he could come to live with me. She said that she had raised him for a long time, and I would need to give her a dress or something in exchange. I bought her a Gomez (Ugandan dress) and a small cow. She was very happy, and David came home with me.

David, 1995

I was thrilled to be able to help the forlorn little boy, but David, on the other hand, was scared to death and cried and cried. I questioned whether I had done the right thing by taking him from his grandmother, because the crying five-year-old tore at my heart. After about two days, he adjusted, and I took him to a doctor who informed me that David suffered from severe malnutrition, so I nourished him back to health with help from Christine and her mother, Margaret.

When David realized that I was going to feed him, his crying subsided, but he was not so sure about the regular baths I insisted on. He was even shy about hugs, but he let me hug him anyway, and then he'd smile.

Those first days provided multiple challenges for us because we did not know how to talk to one another. He didn't know any English, and I didn't know Lugwere, except for common greetings. He pointed at a frog and named it; I told him what it was in English. Then he pointed at more and more things, telling me what they were in Lugwere and me telling him in English. Over time, he learned English, but I still struggle with the local languages. Five of the fifty-two languages are spoken in the village of Kamonkoli, even though English is the official language.

One time when David was ten, he saw the movie *It's a Bug's Life* where the grasshoppers were mean to the ants and made them get food for them. David was touched by this and decided to find out if it was true. He caught a grasshopper and put it in an ants' nest, but the ants killed the grasshopper. Thinking it must be a mistake, he caught another grasshopper, put it in the ants' nest, and the same thing happened. David came in and told me the movie was a lie. "Why do they make a lie?" he asked.

I explained that it was just a story to show how bad bullying is. Of course, I also had to explain what bullying was. David exclaimed, "I hate that movie. I don't like watching things that lie to me!" He had a good and practical understanding of Ephesians 4:25, which says, *Therefore each of you must put off falsehood and speak truthfully to his neighbor, for we are all members of one body.*

David was a lot of fun and I loved him as my own. I carried him with me everywhere I went, and he became the person who was next to me all the time. He was the first living, breathing bundle of hope to walk the paths of Uganda with me. He enjoyed going along when I went evangelizing, and even though he didn't always understand everything, he found it to be fun.

Sometimes we went to town (Mbale) together to buy groceries. We sat on the same boda together and put our food in boxes on another. The trip took about forty minutes by boda.

In my second year, I worked on writing a proposal for an orphanage, thinking this might be the best way to present my mission work to people and churches who wanted to know what I was doing. I gave it to the Presbyterian Church in Uganda, and they turned it over to a visitor from Houston who was part owner of an oil company. He took it and started building it without telling me until much later. I was happy to see the work and know that the proposal was being used, but his interest was in a different part of Uganda from where the Lord had placed my heart.

During this time, another missionary, who was assigned to a main church in the town of Mbale, had come to work with many of the churches on the eastern side of Uganda.. He confronted me face to face, because he did not like seeing a woman in the mission field alone. "This is not of God," he told me.

I responded, "It only makes sense that God would use a woman to help other women and children. A woman can be their mother and love them. God is their Father."

He argued that people were taking advantage of me and using me for their personal gain. These objections had never even crossed my mind. However, as I preached the gospel, I encouraged new converts to be baptized as a confession of their faith. This was also troublesome to that denomination and got me in trouble.

I prayed about this situation, desiring to obey God in all things. In the end, I submitted to his authority, went to Kampala, and worked in another village.

Chapter Eleven

Birth of a Ministry

And we know that in all things God works for the good of those who love him, who have been called according to his purpose. Romans 8:28

Being forced to move to Kampala for nine months was difficult, but God used this time to help me grow, and I learned to depend on Him more than ever. My faith grew stronger and I became friends with the missionary who requested this and his wife.

At first, I wasn't allowed to take David, but they realized they couldn't get me to go without him. I left my home that the people had built for me and went to stay with Grace Kirya in Kampala. She was a widow who had suffered much and whose late husband had been the minister in charge of security for the whole country, reporting directly to his Excellency, President Yoweri Museveni. Grace was and is a wonderful Christian lady. Though this was a very difficult, disappointing time, the Lord taught me about the culture and the country during my time with Grace.

Grace in Kampala, 1996

David was distraught over the move. My being upset probably upset him more, and he didn't adjust well. The city was big, scary, and strange to him. Eventually, I sent him back to Kamonkoli to stay with Christine in our house until I found a way to return or until the Lord moved me back. The separation was difficult for him also, because he was afraid they were going to take him away from me, but after he started school, he was happier.

Whenever possible, I went to visit David on weekends, but Kampala is far from Kamonkoli. I had to catch a bus or taxi, which took about ten hours on very dusty roads. After I got to Kamonkoli, I usually walked or took a boda boda to my house. Then we'd have time to hang out together and go to Saturday Sunday school. Sometimes I would bring something special for David, like a chocolate bar or new tee shirt, and he would smile big. He was always so happy to see me. The Presbyterian Church was okay with these weekend visits, which gave David the security he needed. However, every time I'd get ready to return to Kampala, I found him with his little suitcase, packing to go with me.

A small village outside Kampala called Nachatokolo was my assigned work place during this time. I walked three miles every day to the taxi park to catch a taxi van to Natete, where I waited for another taxi van to take me to Nachatokolo. After I got there, I still had to walk a mile to the school where I worked with orphans and the Presbyterian Church of Nachatokolo.

Realizing that I needed a different supporting church, I sought out the Baptist missionaries. My heart was back at Kamonkoli, and I wanted to return. Grace taught me that it is always wise to wait on the Lord, as the Scriptures teach us. So, I waited and learned as time passed. I also learned about submission to authority, something I had only experienced with my dad, but Ephesians 5:21 gives a broader concept of submission: *Submit to one another out of reverence for Christ.* This incorporates the whole church, the Body of Christ.

David going with Mom

God also taught me about witchcraft during this time. This evil created a great problem in Uganda that I had not been aware of before. Child sacrifice is common, and children sometimes fear being taken away, because their heads are worth a lot of money to the witches. One child's head goes for $300. This was so unbelievable to me and hard to fathom that anyone could want to hurt one of these children. Many young girls believe they can make a man love them with a potion, and men complain when they think they have been bewitched. In Nachatokolo, witchcraft was common. I had never encountered it before, so I sought the help of the Holy Spirit and studied what the Bible had to say about it.

Kampala Taxi Park

All of this witchcraft seemed like a joke to me at first, and I believed that these people were just too skeptical. I now know that the powers of darkness are real and very much at work. I have come to learn that here in Uganda and Africa, these powers are more easily seen than they are in places like Europe or America.

Time passed and I couldn't find any organization that would allow me to return to Kamonkoli to live and work for the Lord. All of the mission agencies wanted me to live in Kampala or Jinja and have no children. I didn't believe that was what the

Lord called me to do in Uganda, so I didn't accept work with them. Though I loved each of these groups as brothers and sisters, I yearned for Kamonkoli. My heart was in Kamonkoli.

One day when I was walking from Grace's home to the taxi park, I was stopped by a little girl. I had been searching to know more about the Holy Spirit at this time when this girl, dressed in a uniform for school, stopped me to say hello and proceeded to tell me she knew me. I asked her how she knew me, because I didn't recognize her. She looked to be about eight years old. She said, "I see you all the time. I even know where you are staying."

I asked her where, and she explained perfectly where I was staying. Then I asked her when we met and told her I was sorry I did not remember. In perfect English, she said, "You will remember later."

I was amazed when this little girl said, "You just don't seem to realize that you know me." She then proceeded to leave.

I turned around to ask her a question, but she was gone. Later I realized that she may have been an angel of the Lord assuring me that I know the Spirit and should not doubt it. That amazing experience encouraged me, and I needed that assurance because with all that had been going on, I felt discouraged and disheartened. This renewed my hope for Kamonkoli and what I felt God's plans were.

Chapter Twelve

Life in the Slums

We are hard pressed on every side, but not crushed;
perplexed, but not in despair; persecuted, but not
abandoned; struck down, but not destroyed. We
always carry around in our body the death of Jesus,
so that the life of Jesus may also be revealed in our
body. 2 Corinthians 4:8-10

After four months of living with Grace, I decided to go and stay with Harriet in the slums where a lot of work needed to be done in evangelizing. Of course, to this day, Grace is still my very dear friend. She was a big help to me with advice and love, and she still is. No one could have been a better Auntie, as they say in Uganda. She spent time with me every day in devotions and with the children staying in her home. Some wealthy Christians came to stay with her from time to time, because they had known her husband and were usually involved in business in Uganda, like safari camps or rubies.

On the other hand, Harriet was like a good sister to me. We laughed together, did a morning and evening devotional study, and prayed together. Harriet lived close to the taxi park too, and I didn't have to walk so far. By the time I came to stay with her, I had holes in the bottom of my shoes and no money to buy new ones.

Harriet

Harriet and I carried water up the stairs to our one room place and cooked on small camping type stoves. We lived on little food; I usually had a sweet bun for breakfast, and at dinner we cooked rice and beans or beef with potatoes. Occasionally we had chicken, but it was too expensive to have often. We ate lots of noodles with avocadoes, because they were cheap. A rat kept coming and swimming in our so-called toilet, which was hard to use with no running water. However, we poured water into it and made it work. Living there wasn't easy, but it offered a chance to share with many people. Several who came to Christ still follow the Lord.

After some time of living in the slums with Harriet, two of my friends in Colorado sent word that they were getting married and wanted to start an organization for the ministry I wanted to do in Kamonkoli. We would form a non-government organization of our own in Uganda and begin this orphanage. I visited many orphanages to see what was being done, what the cost was, and how they were designed. My work with the consulting divisions at Coopers & Lybrand helped in this effort. God knew what kind of training I would need years before, and I was able to use those skills to aid me in this project. Even so, it took almost a year to get all the paper work in place. But after getting the non-profit for Fourth Cross Ministries in place in America and getting a Non-Government Organization (NGO) set up in Uganda, I acquired a new work permit under our own NGO. This meant I was free to return to Kamonkoli.

I checked with the Presbyterian Church, however, to make sure they would be all right with this. I had given nine months to the church in Nachatokolo, had many friends there, and loved the people. I still keep in touch with many and hope that I have encouraged them. But my heart had always stayed in Kamonkoli, and I believed that God wanted me there.

We were encouraged in the fact that God is faithful, and He gave hope to us all. I was encouraged too, when I saw the response of the people of Kamonkoli. About eighty women greeted me at my home, and we sang and praised the Lord. Even children came to celebrate.

Oh, the joy that filled my heart! I was very happy as we rejoiced, and David declared that God was good, and he cried and laughed at the same time. He hugged me and would not let go of my hand. He kept saying, "Are you going to stay now for sure?" Yes, David was the happiest (besides me). Mom was home!

Chapter Thirteen

Home Again

The Lord watches over the alien and sustains the fatherless and the widow, but he frustrates the ways of the wicked. Psalm 146:9

What a thrill to be back home! Yes, Kamonkoli had become my home where I was in love with the people, the land, and the children. But most of all, I was serving my Lord Jesus Christ and developing a sponsorship program here. By this time, however, I had already lived in Uganda for over a year and needed to return to the States for a few months to settle business affairs and raise funds.

After that state-side visit, I returned to Kamonkoli and moved back to the little house they had built for me, which had a designated kitchen area where I could use my kerosene cook stoves. They had added on to a servants' quarters to give me three bedrooms and an inside bathing room that consisted of a cement slab and plastic basin. The jerry cans were my source of water.

Water is a big problem in Uganda. Most people do not have

water near their homes and have to walk a great distance to get to a borehole. When they get it, it is often not clean because the boreholes have not been sunk deep enough. I am surprised at how many boreholes are only fifty to eighty feet, which is not deep enough. Typhoid becomes a problem with contaminated water from such wells.

I am thankful our water was from deep boreholes at the orphanage. It made our lives easier and better. We just had to pump it into the can from a borehole and carry the heavy yellow twenty-liter cans back to the house. Once the water was procured, I poured it from the can into the plastic basin, took a plastic cup, filled it, and poured water all over me. That was my shower. If I wanted it warm, I would heat the water in a kettle on the kerosene stove and then mix it with cold water in the basin.

Gone were the days of long, warm showers to ease sore muscles and soak the grit and grime from my skin. Instead, cup by cup, I washed and rinsed the dust and dirt from my body, but it was inside and I was home. I think washing my hair was the hardest part, as the Lord gave me lots of hair!

Soon after my return, two more children joined me in my home – Christine's little sister Diana and Julius Bumba. Diana didn't like being separated from me and wanted to stay in my home. Her parents didn't seem to care whether she stayed with me or not; they probably felt she had a good future with me. My emotions ruled the day, and I decided to take her in. I loved her and had no regrets.

Julius Bumba had greater needs when he came. His life had been rough for such a young boy. Both of his parents died from AIDS by the time he was seven years old. After his mother died, he heard his relatives talking about where they would take him, and he did not want to go. He knew he had an aunt somewhere in Kamonkoli, so he ran away and kept running until he found

Kamonkoli. He settled into our church building, which was just a shack made from papyrus with a grass roof at that time. He slept there for the night, but Pastor Charles found him in the morning, curled up in the corner of the church.

Julius was scared at first, but he spoke to the pastor and told him who he was, where he had come from, and who he was looking for. But Julius did not know his aunt's name. His aunt turned out to be a lady named Esther, who had been a widow for a very long time but had managed to raise her son Michael, our clinic officer today, by herself with little help. She did not have enough income to raise another child, and her husband had passed away a year after Michael was born, so Julius only stayed with her for one year. Then, in 1997, he came to live with me.

With Diana and Julius, we now had three children in our home, but David was a friendly boy who had many little friends. Living close by, Dick became one of his best friends, and they loved climbing trees together. Dick's father was Islamic and had a few wives, but he abandoned this little boy and left him with his uncle. The father seemed to have more children than he could care for.

I began a Saturday Sunday school by inviting the children who lived around me. At first about twenty children came, but it grew from there. Olive helped me, as we sat on the ground and sang, and I'd share the gospel. The children learned to do skits that we could share with other children. Then we sang more and played games. What a fun time we had, and word spread quickly about our school. We met under one of the cashew nut trees, a big tree with lots of shade. Often sixty to a hundred children came. By the second year, we were up to 150 children or more every Saturday morning.

Dick always came to sing, learn about Jesus, and have fun, and he never missed because he enjoyed it so much. One day he came to me with David and said, "Momma Katherine, I want to know this Jesus too. If He died for me and is living with God, then I should know him too."

I prayed with Dick, and he let out a big laugh and said now he knows he will go to heaven. I told him the prayer was just the beginning, and we must grow with our Lord, learn His Scriptures, and stay close to Him to have this relationship. He ran to tell his friends about it. His next request was a Bible. He told me that even if he could not read all of it, at least he could know that it was the Word of God, and it would make him feel closer to Jesus.

One day when I went to Kampala for paper work on the non-government organization (NGO), Dick and David and some of their other friends played outside while Christine was at home. Dick saw a mean-looking dog that scared him, so he ran as fast as he could. David just froze. When the dog chased Dick, David ran to Dick's uncle for help.

Dick could not run fast enough, and the dog caught up and bit him. Two other children were also bit that day. This dog had rabies, but with no phones in the area, they could not call for help. By the time I returned, about ten days later, Dick had died a terrible death. The other two boys had died as well. They had suffered terrible pain, but no one could help them.

They told me Dick had been asking for me. He told everyone, "If Momma Katherine were here to pray for me, I know I could get all better." Then he asked David and Christine to tell me "bye" and he would see me in heaven. I cried as much as I would have for my own children. David cried too. After the funeral, I was stunned to find out there was no treatment for rabies anywhere in Mbale or Uganda except in Entebbe, a twelve-hour drive at this time because of the dirt roads.

The loss of Dick impressed upon me, more than ever, the great need for better medical care in the area. Margaret's mud hut clinic could not address the severe problems the Ugandans faced. I realized we needed to pray about this and looked into getting help, because the medical conditions were far worse than I could ever have imagined.

The church allowed me to evangelize after I returned, so I went out several times during the week, usually with Olive. She had become a close friend, as well as Christine and Harriet. I also worked with Margaret, the mother of these three. God was using me as I spoke to the people, and the church grew and more people came to know Christ. Believing we needed Bible studies, I started with the women and began meeting every week. Pastor Charles and I also started a discipleship class with new converts, meeting for six months with each group. Even though I was not trained in all of this, I felt God's Spirit leading me. We often stopped just to pray with people.

Sometimes I preached in a Pentecostal church in Jami, another part of the village of Kamonkoli. Two boys, Duchu and Henry, had lost their parents, but they sang in that church every Sunday and were good little boys who caught the eyes of the people. I grew fond of them and learned more about their lives.

Duchu was a stubborn but sweet youngster. He could not understand why God would let both of his parents die and make him live with his uncle, a witch doctor in the area, who kept snakes in some of his shrines for his evil rituals. Neither of the boys wanted to stay with the uncle, so I finally took them to a little house on our property to live with one of our workers, a staff member for HUM. As Duchu got older, he was much like me – always wondering why he was here, what was the reason for living. He tried to kill himself one time, and we recognized how much he was struggling. After a lot of loving and counseling, he changed and accepted Christ into his life. Then, everything changed for him.

Duchu did well in school and won a scholarship to the university through the government. He attended Makerere University where he earned his degree in Business Management. Now he is running East African Harvest Ministries and pastoring his church – Revival Harvest Ministries – in a bad slum of Mbale. Duchu is married to Aisha, and they are expecting their first child, as they learn about finding sponsors for the children in the church.

Goma helping mom pack for visitation

My family grew with each addition of children, but one day I got a baby – literally. Goma was very young, not even a year, when he came to live with me. He was a joy and the brother of Israel, who is not his real brother, but they always played and stayed together since they were very small. Sometimes we called them the twins.

They liked to follow me around and insisted on going everywhere with Mommy. Goma, however, wanted me to hold him a lot, and whenever he went, Israel had to go. They liked watching cartoons, because by this time I had a television and DVD player. They loved power rangers, but I was not sure I did at all. They said when they grew up, they were going to be power rangers. Now, they are not interested and wonder what was wrong with them.

They loved football and enjoyed playing with all the little kids who live outside the orphanage; every day you will find many children in our compound playing football. They enjoyed sharing and giving away any clothes that no longer fit them. Today they are both in their fourth year of high school and Jinja College, and both know the Lord Jesus Christ as their Lord and Savior and are always eager to learn more about the Bible.

Boys circumcised

A time came when I realized that most of the boys in my home were not circumcised. How did I know? In Kamonkoli a ritual takes place every other year when boys are circumcised at about the age of thirteen and older. They are stripped in public and circumcised with a knife that is usually dull and dirty. They say this marks the time the boy becomes a man. They put on grass skirts and paint their bodies and faces with strange looking marks; then they parade around dancing with crowds following and screaming for joy with them.

Not only is this painful for the boys, but it is not biblical, so I teach the children about this in Sunday school. They learn how and why circumcision started in the Old Testament. One day I realized I should take my boys to the doctor to be circumcised or they might end up in one of the rituals. I hated seeing them in pain, but they were funny walking around in their grass skirts, laughing and joking about being men.

Young David (not my first David) came about this time and was a joy. He was circumcised by his mother at the age of eight days. He came when his mother was working for me as a nanny. David was quite destructive as a child, but funny as could be. What's not to love.

Chapter Fourteen

Some Live, Some Die

My days have passed, my plans are shattered, and so are the desires of my heart. These men turn night into day; in the face of darkness they say, "Light is near." Job 17:11-12

One time when I was out evangelizing, some children called me to come to their house. I went with Olive and found a very sick, extremely thin, teenage boy with sores all over his body. They told me John was dying, probably from AIDS. He took my hand and said, "Pray for me. I know if you pray for me, I can get better."

I told him that only God had the ability to heal, but I would pray for God to do that. As I was praying, I felt that God was giving me a message for John. I told him, "God will heal you to go out and share the gospel, but on the day you decide to stop preaching the gospel or telling others what God has done for you, how He sent His Son to die on the cross for you, and raised Him from the dead, you will again be sick and die."

John did indeed get up the next day and begin to preach,

because *He commanded us to preach to the people and to testify that he is the one whom God appointed as judge of the living and the dead* (Acts 10:42). He told everyone, and many came to believe in Jesus because they had seen John moving when they thought he was dead for sure. He continued this for a few years, and then one day I heard he stopped preaching.

The people kept telling me, "It was just like you said. When he stopped preaching, he died." I cried for him but was thankful that he had preached for at least two years, and I knew he died a believer.

By this time, I had a little girl named Violet. Her father had died when she was three years old, and her mother, Esther, was very sick with AIDS and tuberculosis (TB). TB is common with those who have AIDS in Africa, because their immune system is so weak. Esther had come to know Christ and asked me to take at least one of her six children, preferably Violet, her youngest daughter. So, I took Violet in.

At first, Violet didn't know what to expect in my home. One day she dropped a glass, and it broke. Seeing the glass shards took me back to the day I dropped the Prell bottle and saw my mom in the hospital, as broken, unfixable glass. The Lord had brought me beyond the shattered glass and healed my heart, but Violet was scared. She ran and hid.

I went to Esther to find out if Violet had come home, but she had not seen her. She helped me search, and we found her hiding in a bush. She was crying and scared, so I asked Esther why she would be scared so suddenly. I related to her about the glass, and Esther explained that in the past she would have received a beating for this. I asked her why, and she did not know the answer, but it was the culture that when a child breaks something, they must be disciplined.

I told Violet that she should not be afraid, and I knew she didn't do it on purpose. Promising not to beat her, I asked her to come out of the bush. Julius, David, and Diana were all trying to coax her out of the bush, but it took an hour of such coaxing before she finally emerged, ran up to me, and put her arms around me. I just hugged her and cried silently.

Violet settled into my home and enjoyed living with me, but within nine months, her mother died. That was a very hard time for Violet who was one of my most sensitive children. I helped to bury her mother and then held Violet tightly, as David and Julius cried with her. We were all accustomed to Esther coming over all the time, and we loved her. She knew Christ and was active in the women and widow's ministry, sharing the gospel and telling others of the love of Christ for them.

Esther Naula's Grave

Animals

Uganda is not necessarily a safe place to live, or should I say, the dangers are different from those in the United States. Many animals live in Africa – elephants, giraffes, lions, leopards, and all kinds of monkeys and chimpanzees. I have never gone to the park where there are gorillas because it is too expensive – $575 a day for tracking gorillas, without food or lodging.

Sometimes the teams that come want to go on safari and take us with them. When a team visits Uganda, they are under the care of the NGO for Hines Ugandan Ministries. Once I went to Queen Elizabeth National Park with them, and before we checked in to get a guide, we saw elephants. We were so excited by those magnificent animals that Diane and I hopped out of the van and slowly walked toward them. Closer and closer we walked. Silly me, I thought elephants were always friendly like those in the zoo.

Six big ones stood there. Then they turned, faced us, and trumpeted. With the sound of their trumpet, they charged straight toward us. Scared to death, we turned and sprinted, but Diane's knees hurt and she wanted to stop for a bit. We stopped behind a bush, but when the elephants trumpeted again, we took off running. The elephants stopped, turned, and went back the way they had come. But for the grace of God and His watchfulness, we would have become the new stomping ground for those gray giants. Our brush with that deadly danger taught me not to mess with the animals.

However, one time I had a close call with a lion. I was sitting on the back of a truck, taking pictures of a male and female lion under a tree – about thirty feet away. As I was zooming in with my camera, the driver decided to move, and the truck bounced me off the back, but one leg got caught. As the truck moved closer for better pictures, I was being dragged in front of the lions. They kept looking at me, wondering if I was dinner, so I tried not to make any noise for fear they would see me as a threat. Finally, I got my foot loose and jumped back onto the truck. The guide realized what had happened just as I got my foot out and he nearly had a heart attack. He jumped out with his gun ready to shoot, but he didn't because with two lions, one might jump while he shot at the other. Fortunately, God kept those lions from attacking us, and we got away safely.

The King

Baboons live near our house, so when visitors come who do not have much time, we take those people to see the baboons and feed them. We combine it with a trip to view the beautiful waterfalls on top of the mountain. This makes an exciting one-day excursion for these people.

Often monitor lizards can be found behind our house. These huge creatures have long necks, powerful tails, and claws and are not safe around children because they are carnivorous, eating eggs, smaller reptiles, fish, birds, and small mammals. The adult length of some of them can be over ten feet, but many are smaller. I used to be concerned when David and the other children would play there.

Backyard Cobra

Even worse, however, are the cobra snakes. The king cobras seem to pass through the yard once or twice a year when they are looking for water. They are among the most venomous snakes on the planet. They can reach a length of eighteen feet, and when confronted, they can raise up vertically to face their enemy and hiss like a growling dog. Once our cat, Boo Boo, decided to fight with a big one, about thirteen feet long, but the snake chose to escape.

Sickness

Being bombarded with death and sickness all around me and striving to meet the needs of malnourished and starving children, I sometimes forgot or neglected my own needs. One time this carelessness caught up with me.

At first, we thought I had malaria and I was treated for it, even though my test came back negative. Sometimes early in such a disease, the tests run negative but turn positive later. I had a headache and flu like symptoms, which is very common to malaria. A week went by with no improvement, just that continual flu feeling – weak and feverish. We knew then that I did not have malaria; typhoid fever was the offender.

Margaret, our nurse at the clinic, and Michael, our present Medical Officer, treated me at home. They started an IV to keep me from being dehydrated, because I was not able to keep food or fluids down. When I lifted my head from the bed, the room spun around and around. I would throw up and lie back down I was so dizzy. Even the bed spun around. In desperation, I'd shut my eyes and cry out to God to help me.

My fever raged dangerously high at 103° to 104°, sometimes reaching 105°. Margaret kept cold compresses on me to help cool my body, but she feared I would die anyway. After two weeks, however, the spinning subsided and I recovered – quite a few pounds lighter. God, the Great Physician, still had work for me to do.

Typhoid fever was indeed the culprit, for I had failed to keep up with my vaccinations, which left me vulnerable. Uganda suffers from typhoid, which is the number one illness we treat at the clinic. Though it is not contagious from person to person, it is contracted from bacteria in bad water. Bacteria – such a tiny thing that can inflict so much trouble.

Chapter Fifteen

Grief and Joy

I tell you the truth, you will weep and mourn while
the world rejoices. You will grieve, but your grief
will turn to joy. John 16:20

One day some children came running to get me from home. Fear exploded from their faces, as they described the screaming lady who needed help right away. I hurried as fast as I could and found a pregnant woman with a very high fever. We rushed to the Marah Medical Center, which had two rooms for clinic use but found them locked because Margaret had gone to town to get some drugs.

This lady was seven months pregnant but had gone into premature labor from the high fever. Even though she had malaria, she did not take the medicine for fear of harming the baby. I gave her some aspirin and a glass of clean water because I did not know what else I could do. Then I sent David and Violet home for a couple bottles of water, some towels, scissors (they came with a knife), and a jerry can filled with hot water.

When they returned, the baby was on its way, and we could

not make it to a clean room anywhere. I tore a thread from my slip and used it to tie the umbilical cord. The baby cried, which was good, and I cleaned it with the lukewarm bottled water and wrapped it in towels, but it was too small, probably only about three pounds.

I cleaned the mother up as well as I could out in the bush and took her to the guesthouse where David and Violet were helping get the bed ready. She slept for a while, and when she awoke, I gave her some food. Margaret had returned and checked out the baby, stating that it needed to be extra warm. We knew that without an incubator the baby might die.

Margaret treated the mother's malaria and hooked up an IV; she seemed to be getting stronger by the next day but had no milk for the baby. We mixed up some milk, and the little baby took it and seemed to be doing okay.

Later, the lady's husband came, and he was furious that I was taking care of the baby. He said, "That baby should be killed. It will give us problems all the days of our lives."

I could not understand this thinking, so I said, "You want me to kill an innocent baby?" I had never heard of such a thing and told him not to be so harsh on the child. I told him, "I will help you when there are problems. Please do not harm the baby."

When he seemed to calm down, I went for a car to transport them to the hospital and was only gone ten minutes. When I returned, the baby was dead. My floodgates opened wide and tears gushed from my eyes once more. I could not talk to the husband or his wife, as I was so distraught. To make it worse, they had named the girl Katherine. I turned and fled as fast as I could.

Sometime later, I visited them in their home and shared the gospel with them. That particular wife came to Christ (he had more than one wife). They were Islamic but not strong in their beliefs. Before he died, though, the husband gave his life to Christ. One never knows when the seeds that are planted and watered will be harvested. Only God knows, and we do our part by planting and watering. Then we pray for the harvest. When I knew he died a Christian, I rejoiced as I had long ago forgiven him for what he did to the baby.

Sometimes the things that happen in life do not make sense. Sometimes it seems that God asks the impossible. When life seems unfair, or you see so much death, so much suffering, so much pain, and so many tears, you wonder. I have found that joy comes at the end of it, as Paul writes: *May the God of hope fill you with all joy and peace as you trust in him, so that you may overflow with hope by the power of the Holy Spirit* (Romans 15:13). For those in Christ, joy comes. Like Job in the Bible who was rich with a big family, but then he lost it all. However, he never left God or never cursed Him in any way, and in the end, he was more than restored with joy – total joy and peace. God used it for His glory, and it worked to the good of others as well.

Chapter Sixteen

Slow Progress

Give generously to him and do so without a grudging heart; then because of this the Lord your God will bless you in all your work and in everything you put your hand to. Deuteronomy 15:10

Coming from a fast-paced country, I had to adjust to how long everything took and how difficult and slow any work was done. Accomplishing things had been much different when I lived in America. As a finance administrator for a large accounting firm, I did budgets and more for seven offices and accounting for the consulting division. What a difference Uganda was from working in an air-conditioned building on the 34th floor with a wonderful view of Denver and having many deadlines in a fast-paced atmosphere.

One time I went to get money from the Ugandan bank account I had set up. After I waited nearly four hours, I asked if there was a problem, or was something wrong? The man told me that his boss had stepped out, and no one else could approve the transaction.

I was exhausted from the trip and tired of waiting. I told him I needed to get funds from my account. Then I cried. That took care of it, and he said he would take responsibility for it and gave me my funds. The poor man felt sorry for me.

I wondered sometimes how much time is wasted waiting for anything and everything. When I was going to meet with some women and children, I had to tell them to come two hours prior to the time I wanted them to come because they were always about two hours late. So, if we were going to meet at nine, I asked them to come at seven. At times when I was waiting, I would think the Lord would return before we even got started at the meeting. I remember Mexican time, but Uganda has them beat.

Transportation

I had no vehicle my first four years in Uganda and either rode in a taxi van, on the back of a boda boda, or I walked. In those early years, I walked an average of three to four miles a day – and, oh, it kept me skinny.

My first car was a Nissan Sunny, about eighteen years old and barely able to run, but it helped for a while. Then I bought a truck for $10,000 that was supposed to have been refurbished with a new engine. What a joke!

One day, Olive and I were driving in the village when the truck decided to quit running. We knew that often the problem was just loose wires, so we got duct tape out to try to remedy the situation. This truck sat quite high off the ground, so we climbed up on the fenders and leaned over the engine – not too stable of a position. We made quite a sight as we teetered over the truck engine and practically fell in, trying to find something to tape together.

Someone saw us, came over, and asked what we were doing. They laughed at the silly sight of us balancing on top of the truck, obviously not knowing what we were doing. Then the children also gathered around and laughed, so we started singing and laughing with them. After some time, Pastor Charles rescued us and joined in the singing. He shared the gospel with them also and several accepted Christ as their Savior. In the end, I had to get a proper engine put in the truck, and it served us for seven years.

On some occasions, Olive and I would have a problem with it, and we'd stop to try to figure it out. Once I got the duct tape and taped some wires to see if it would work. It did, for a little bit, but then the starter burned out. Having a working vehicle was a constant challenge.

Modern conveniences

No phones were available for my first six years, so I had to go all the way to Kampala to make a phone call to the States to ask for money to be wired. That was an eight- to ten-hour drive in a hot taxi van overstuffed with people and things – like chickens, goats, and whatever – and upon arrival, I would be covered in red dust. Because of the long trip, I left early enough to get to the post office before it would close, so I could use the one phone for an outside AT&T operator to call collect to the States. Such a transfer of funds usually took two to three weeks. Then I would stay in the slums with Harriet for the night.

I had no running water until January 2001, when it first started to come in my area. I quickly had a good toilet and bath-tub installed – for the first time since I had come to Uganda. This running water lasted about four months before it was turned off for about six months. Then it was turned back on and fortunately left on.

Electricity was always an on and off affair. At first, my little house did not have electricity, but after putting it in, it was off, then on, and so it goes every day. In the beginning they had a load-shedding schedule of three hours every other night when there was a deliberate shutdown to prevent failure of the entire system. I am not sure what the time off in between was called. Later in 2008 and 2009 we had twenty-four hours off every other day because they had overloaded the dam. Then a new dam was built, but we are still on and off. Uganda is landlocked, so in the 1950s the English made a deal to sell electricity to Kenya in order to use the borders. Electricity has never improved in Uganda and is terribly expensive for terrible service.

My first stove arrived in January 2001 when my first mission team came to visit me and bought one for me. I was thrilled as Christine and I had been cooking on those little camping stoves for a long time. I received a refrigerator that same month. It was like having Christmas five times after the New Year had begun. We rejoiced that day and praised God for providing wonderful gifts to make our lives easier.

Discouragement & Hope

Coming to Uganda to love the children was not as easy as I thought it should be and would be. I did not expect so much trouble from the Devil himself, but my ministry did not make him happy, and he confused and disorganized at every turn. As soon as the ministry started gaining ground, and people were coming to the Lord, something would happen that did not seem possible.

Many times the loneliness closed in on me as I longed for fellowship. Many nights I stayed up and cried to the Lord for help. Many times we had no funds and lived month to month, trusting the Lord to bring what we needed. Sometimes we fell short, and I cried to the Lord, *Turn to me and be gracious to me, for I am lonely and afflicted* (Psalm 25:16). I survived by faith, because I knew I was called to do this. I was groomed by the Lord to do His work: my past had prepared me for my work in Uganda, and what the Lord starts, He is able to finish.

Even now, I look around me and see that the children are not cared for. They are not taught – many never go to school. Their parents are dying, and where I live in the Budaka District, at least one of every three adults is dying of AIDS. They say it is getting better, but it is hard to see. We have funerals every week where children are burying their parents. What will happen to these children? Usually they are shuffled between relatives, often treated as slaves, working for their food and bed. Seldom are they loved, but the children need love, the kind of love that can only come from the Lord and the people He sends.

People often ask what a typical day is like in Uganda as a missionary. We have no typical days. I get up early in the morning to pray and spend some time alone with our Lord as often as it is possible. Then I see my children off to school and head for the office. Sometimes I do not have a routine, as someone may come seeking medical help or solutions to other problems. Sometimes I find myself heading for a hospital instead of a clinic.

The initial ministry that was founded to support our work in Uganda began struggling, and it was clear something had to give. The founders, however, resisted the needed changes."

However, two of the board members and some other supporters stuck with me. In 1999, we incorporated as a non-profit known as Hines Ugandan Ministries (HUM), and I had to re-register everything for the Ugandan NGO. The name "Hines Ugandan Ministries" was chosen so supporters knew they were still supporting the same ministry. This difficult time took six months in the States, but the Lord opened new doors, and we found new donors. It was not easy, but Aunt Grace recommended a lawyer, and he did a good job of setting up the NGO and incorporating, which allowed us to own land.

We bought nine acres to build the orphanage on, but then I

needed to procure a land title so no one could take it away from HUM. Our district did not have a land board, however, so this process did not get finished until November 2004.

In the first month of HUM, we started the child sponsorship program and had nine children sponsored. (When I say we, I am talking of those who were working with me – Olive, Judith, Pastor Charles and Michael.) We finally felt like we were going to make a difference for these young lives. We developed a mission goal of raising children to become Christian leaders who could make a difference to their country and community to the glory of God.

By the end of the year, we had eighty-four children sponsored and a Saturday Sunday school of about two to three hundred every Saturday morning. The women and widow's ministry met every Wednesday for a Bible study, and the women organized a fund where each of them would bring a thousand shillings (about one dollar), and one of them would collect it each month. The group started with twelve, but quickly grew to about sixty. A very serious discipleship class of thirteen men and women also met for a whole year, and those thirteen are now teaching others.

The longer I stayed in Kamonkoli, Uganda, the more I grew to love the children and being a mom. What I lacked, I was not aware of, because I was blessed to be chosen to work with these people and children. I had found the purpose God had for my life. The brokenness, the trials, the troubles, and the shattered glass of my life prepared and strengthened me for His calling – I had a reason to live.

I still wondered what would happen to all of these children, but I am glad that HUM can help some of them. Progress continues as I pray and believe that only the Lord Jesus can bring life and hope to the helpless multitudes who face the shattered glass of their own lives.

My Little Women

My Little Men

Chapter Seventeen

Expansion in the Midst of Danger

And God is able to make all grace abound to you,
so that in all things at all times, having all that you
need, you will abound in every good work.
2 Corinthians 9:8

The political and religious environment in Uganda creates unusual and sometimes dangerous situations to work in. Thankfully, I have only encountered problems with a few Muslims. One was a political leader who hated Christians and wanted the orphanage fence and gate knocked down for a road. He lost, however, and the road was built not only straight through his property, but right through his house. God indeed fought that battle for us.

I can honestly say I have never wished evil on any of these people, but I pray for them that the Holy Spirit might touch their hearts and they might accept Jesus Christ and experience His love.

A few other Muslims have opposed our evangelistic crusades, but we manage to get approval for them anyway. Once, during a crusade, they started fighting with some of our workers, and the fight grew into a larger brawl. We were mostly resisting, but they were fighting.

Because of that conflict, all crusades now require a police presence, and we have to pay them. Al Shabaab, an al-Qaeda-linked militant group based in Somalia, is present in Uganda and always making threats. Therefore, we have to go through security whenever we enter any stores or restaurants, just like an airport. Two restaurants were blown up on July 7, 2010, on the last day of the FIFA World Cup football match. Nearly a hundred people were killed, including Jason, a missionary with Invisible Children, who worked in the Gulu area with the Lost Children.

In the midst of such turmoil, progress to make a difference and develop our sponsorship program with HUM was slow, but the ministries for the women and children grow in spite of the chaos surrounding us. Our Saturday Sunday school has become the AWANA Clubs for children. Through missionary friends in Kampala, we discovered that AWANA was present in Uganda, and I could get books and materials from them. After contacting them, we hosted the Club in Pastor Charles' Presbyterian Church, which was much better than under the big cashew tree.

Today, about three hundred children come every Saturday, and during the holidays when school is out, that number grows to eight hundred and even over a thousand. These excited children can have fun and learn about the Lord as they memorize Scriptures, thereby writing God's Word in their hearts, *for the word of God is living and active. Sharper than any double-edged sword, it penetrates even to dividing soul and spirit, joints and marrow; it judges the thoughts and attitudes of the heart* (Hebrews 4:12). This builds a lasting faith foundation for them as they prepare to lead and have a global impact.

An AWANA Christmas Celebration

After my recent trip back to the United States (2015), we had a big Christmas celebration for the children. Like all children, they love holidays and came out in full force – 1,390 of them. Rented tents provided some protection from the sun and helped keep the children together. About a hundred of our youth became helpers along with our fifteen AWANA teachers, and the children were well behaved and orderly.

AWANA under the trees

AWANA fun

AWANA children studying verses

2015 Christmas party

They started arriving around 9:00 a.m., and by 9:30 a.m. when I arrived, almost 300 children were ready and waiting. By 10:00 a.m. over a thousand had arrived. Each team member taught the Christmas story to a group of children, along with the popular Candy Cane story, as we always incorporate the purpose of Christ coming in every Bible story that we teach.

This year our craft was the making of an ornament by using a bent pipe cleaner and stringing white and red beads on it until it looked like a candy cane. This went well with the telling of the Candy Cane story and gave the children something to take home where they probably had no other ornaments. Then we played trivia during our game time, and one little boy, Cliff, answered a hard question and won several sweet treats, much to his delight. All of the children get a sweet for answering questions, and in Uganda, a sweet is like a treasure.

With so many children, we had to break into groups with different helpers and periodically rotate for variety. The children were so happy to be there that they were quite patient when they had to wait. Besides, they knew they would also receive a good hot meal and cake. Three cooks prepared the food for us as they do for every party we have; they served rice, cabbage, beans, and beef. A lady in town who makes cakes for weddings and other functions made sixteen cakes for us. Each child received a small piece and some candy. A precious memory for me was seeing one little girl, Mercy Katherine, who was standing by the cake, looking up with those big eyes and waiting for some cake to eat.

Along with the craft, games, and food, we had music – lots of music. Three of our youth were in charge of playing music and running the sound system, but we do not have accompaniment instruments – just lots of singing and dancing. We had regular Christmas music and some traditional Christmas music sung by African groups. The children's choir performed a few songs, and we had a dance contest. Even the staff and team members joined in the contest – everyone here loves music and dancing.

Finally, after a good, fun-filled day with lots of food and entertainment, the party ended and the children all headed home. Best of all, they had experienced love and joy, and the craft they took home could remind them of a Savior who shed His blood for them, giving them hope for the future.

Other Services

In addition to AWANA, many other services are developing in our area, including a medical clinic, a primary school, a craft center that also sews uniforms for the schools, a small orphanage with four houses, and the sponsorship programs. We take children when they are very young and care for and teach them until they have finished either the university or vocational school. We continue with the students after high school because they do not yet have the skills to get a job. To stop training after high school would be like taking them back to the village to sit and do nothing. Besides, when the Lord asks me to do something, I do not want to go half way or part of the way. I believe we should finish what we start.

God has blessed us with other compassionate, faithful people to join in our work. One time in Lakeland, Florida, I was visiting sponsors I had never met. They had sponsored children because their daughter had met me and convinced them to join the sponsorship program. They, in turn, introduced me to someone they thought might be a good donor, and he wanted me to meet with the Florida Baptist Childrens' Homes board. I wondered what I would get out of this – how could someone building homes in Florida help me in Uganda?

But God had a plan, and it was His timing. At the meeting, I met Ron Gunter, a sincere humble man of God. I shared the work of HUM with him, and he said I was in luck because Florida Baptist Children's Homes had just decided to go international and start Orphan's Heart. They were interested in collaborating with us when they saw the work the Lord had given us to do. We thank God for that meeting. I was thrilled with the way God put me in touch with such special people.

I did not hear from them for several years however. Even so, Ron had not forgotten, and he contacted me as soon as they were able to look at Africa. Orphan's Heart was a God-send for HUM. We were struggling financially, and they have come along side, supported us with building funds and materials, and even created a refrigerator fund. They help us get sponsors and have advised us on our clinic, school curriculum, and written policies. We work together on the vision the Lord has given us.

Ron and Cynthia of Orphan's Heart

With the expansion of our programs and services, we are able to help so many more needy people. A widow named Joyce went through our discipleship training and joined the women's ministries. She was a sweet, funny lady who brewed liquor, a kind of moonshine, to sell for a living. Then she gave her life to Christ and didn't know what to do. We helped her start a shop, which was working well for her until she died. She had been such a joy, always with a smile on her face, but she had a stomach problem. The doctor seemed to think that it might have been from poison, but he was not sure.

Another lady who came to Christ had two children, but she also had AIDS. Her husband had died a few years earlier after he had given her the virus. He had been unfaithful to her, which is not unusual in Uganda. She gave her life to Christ one day as we prayed, but she had two concerns: The first was, what would happen to her two sons when she died, and the second was how many people she could share the gospel with before she died.

She must have shared with hundreds of other ladies, many of whom came to Christ and changed their lives. She realized that her life had a purpose for God, *for we are God's workmanship, created in Christ Jesus to do good works, which God prepared in advance for us to do* (Ephesians 2:10). Her two sons have been sponsored and have both finished at the university. One is working, and the other is looking for work. However, the two sons have not come to know Christ as their Lord and Savior, though they have heard the gospel many times. Much work still needs to be done and many still need the hope that only Jesus Christ can bring.

Chapter Eighteen

Witchcraft

Finally, be strong in the Lord and in his mighty
power. Put on the full armor of God so that you can
take your stand against the devil's schemes.
Ephesians 6:10-11

Witchcraft is probably the largest religion in Uganda. The witches and witch doctors are similar to wicked Manasseh in the Old Testament who *sacrificed his own son in the fire, practiced sorcery and divination, and consulted mediums and spiritists. He did much evil in the eyes of the Lord, provoking him to anger* (2 Kings 21:6).

In Uganda they have many little huts set up, which they call shrines, but these anger God today as much as in the time of Manasseh. I thank God that He has used me to share the Word with many of them, and some have accepted Christ. However, those still bound in this demonic religion do horrible things and usually get AIDS, because they often take payment in sexual favors.

Most days we hear of a child who has gone missing, and

it turns out they were sacrificed in an evil ritual. The witches sell the heads of children for $300, which is a lot of money to them. They also sacrifice adults, but God says, *Do not give any of your children to be sacrificed* (Leviticus 18:21). This is an abominable thing to God.

My friends and fellow workers taught me much about witchcraft, which has several levels – like a hierarchy. At the top is the Wizard, who gets instructions directly from the Devil, and below the wizards are the witches who take their orders from the Wizard. Below the witches are the witch doctors and then the night dancers. The witch doctors lure people in by making them think they can solve their problems or sicknesses. Some say night dancers dance upside down on their heads at night and deliver curses for the witches. This evil is much more common than most people realize.

One time a witch doctor put a curse on me. For five days I experienced all sorts of problems until I heard about what he had done. I got down on my knees and prayed to God to release me from this curse. Immediately, the problems started going away. However, after two weeks the witch doctor died. This caused the people to fear me, because they knew the Lord was with me, and it is true that greater is He who is in me than he that is in the world.

Florence

Florence was considered the worst witch doctor in the village, and she was definitely the scariest because she had the most power. The first time I went to visit her, I was with a team of people from the States. She wanted me to stay awhile, but I felt the evil the minute I entered her compound. In all her wickedness, even her eyes were dark red and glowing with evil. Of course, the mind can play tricks when you are scared, but we did feel the evil.

Florence's son, Jonah, practiced with her, and they had dead animals hanging up around some of the huts and skins hanging inside the huts. I asked her why she wanted to follow the Devil, and she said he had promised to make her rich and give her everything she could possibly want. She knew her power came from him, so why would she want to leave him. She had done many horrible things, but she was sick with AIDS and tuberculosis. I told her he had lied to her and that only God keeps His promises and cares about her.

Florence looked like the witch in cartoons and movies with the big pot and all. A year later, I returned to her home with one other person, and she finally admitted that I told her the truth – the Devil is a liar. She got down on her knees in the dirt and cried, and I got right down there with her and put my arm around her. She accepted Christ that day.

Florence had many shrines, but she burned them all down to the ground with everything in them. A year later Jonah gave his life to Christ too. The home has changed now, and Florence has received treatment for her diseases. She exhibits the real power of God and even looks different with a true hope in her life. God's love is transforming her, and the Holy Spirit is renewing her. Florence attends the women's Bible study when she is well enough and often attends church. She is living proof of James 4:7, which tells us to *submit yourselves, then, to God. Resist the devil, and he will flee from you.*

Bumbula

Once I moved to the orphanage, I was surrounded by witches – one behind me, one to the right, one to the left, and Bumbula was close by too. The one to the right of me had already given his life to Christ and changed, but the one behind me decided to move because the spirit vibes were "bad." Bumbula, however, kept dodging me. He served many people in the community and had done some terrible things, but his daughter, Desire, came to AWANA and went home and told him he needed to get saved. She told him he needed Jesus and he was going to hell if he continued to serve the Devil. Desire was only three at the time.

The Lord gave me enough courage to go visit him, because I relied on God's Word: *Be self-controlled and alert. Your enemy the devil prowls around like a roaring lion looking for someone to devour. Resist him, standing firm in the faith, because you know that your brothers throughout the world are undergoing the same kind of sufferings* (1 Peter 5:8-9). I had gone many times, but always failed to find Bumbula home. His wife told me he always seemed to know when I was coming, and he'd take off. She said the Devil had spoken to him to make sure he would not be there when I arrived.

One day I prayed for a long time before going, and I took my son Henry with me. We found Bumbula at home, so I shared the gospel and some other Scriptures with him. He broke down and cried with tears streaming down his face and confessed to me; I just listened and cried with him. He told me how three of his children died at the hands of the demons. He believed he was going to get riches and be powerful. "I was so stupid that I allowed the demons to suck the life out of them. I did nothing to stop them."

I asked him if he just feared them, and he said "No, I gave them freely because I was so lost in the evil." As time went by, he missed the children. All of them were young: one was three, one was five, and the other was six – two girls and one boy. Bumbula did not change that day, but he confessed.

A month later, I went to visit him with my daughter Sarah, and he got on his knees with us and cried out to God. I told him that God had forgiven him and he must learn to forgive himself. He could not understand how God could forgive him or how He could still love him, and though he would learn to forgive, he could not forget. I explained that God would help him grow as his heart was changing, and He would help take care of him now.

Today there is a marked difference in the children in that home. Bumbula came to the Lord through a seed that was planted by his little daughter who learned about Jesus at AWANA. She was very bold to share truth with her witch doctor father, but she is now a thriving young Christian in the 4th grade who loves the Lord.

Housemaid

Once, I hired a lady to work in my home as a housemaid, which all missionaries and people here do if they can. It provides a job for someone. This lady had come to me asking for the job, because she knew I was looking for someone to clean and help in the house. I did not know she came from a home of witchcraft. Her mother was a powerful witch and wanted her to join the craft. She had refused and was trying to get away from it.

This lady was with me only one month, however. One day she fell and almost burned down my little kitchen. She said she had lost her sight and felt ill but could not tell me why. I looked at her and told her she should go for a malaria test. I did not understand what was happening at the time.

She said she went for the test, but really just pretended to. Later that same week, she fell on the floor and cried out that she could not stand it any longer. She said she was blind again and they would not let her see until she went home. I was confused about who "they" were and what she was talking about. I called for Pastor Charles, who was my neighbor, and he came and asked her questions. Christine and Michael were there as well. We were all dumbfounded.

Finally, she told us there was too much praying in this house and they could not stand it. I asked her who "they" were and told her to pray with me and ask Jesus to send the "theys" away. She cried and said I should not use that name around her, so Pastor Charles insisted that he had better drive her home. As he reached her home, he discovered the truth: "They" were demons that were fighting her to go back and work with her mother.

A week later my children woke me, saying things were flying around. They all huddled in my bed, crying and asking me to pray, so I did. I went to their room (the girls' room) and discovered a mess. Clothes were flying everywhere. As I entered the room, a book came flying at me.

I saw flowers on the table in the hallway where we ate our meals. I asked where the flowers came from. No one knew.

I ran to the boys' room, which was quiet, but Bumba Julius was missing. I looked all around the house for him, as things continued to fly in the girls' room. This evil made me angry because it had no business in my home, because my home belongs to Jesus. I got on my knees in the girls' room and prayed, and I told the evil spirits to leave this house. I told them Jesus would fight them, and they should know this house belongs to Him. As I prayed, the room became quiet, and the front door opened wide even though it had a padlock on it.

I had never encountered such things before. Bumba came out from under the bed in the girls' room and said he didn't know how he got there. The other boys finally woke up and said they heard nothing.

Apparently, the spirit of this girl had returned and wanted to cause us problems. She returned once again a week later, but with lots of prayer, she left before she created a mess. I was told that sometimes they leave something personal as an "in" to your home. When this lady hurried to gather her things to go home, she had left a petticoat behind. So we burned it, and I knew she would not come back again.

Even though the demonic religion of witchcraft is very powerful, our God has more power. Our God is good and loving, not evil. Our God gives us hope. The Devil does not stand a chance against the God of angel armies and the God of the universe.

Chapter Nineteen

Suffering Families

They were hungry and thirsty, and their lives ebbed away. Then they cried out to the Lord in their trouble and he delivered them from their distress.
Psalm 107:5-6

Lovista

Our Saturday Sunday school (AWANA) allowed us to meet the children who needed the most help. Lovista was one of those who came to learn and play games with the other children. She was a little girl when I met her, just five years old like my David. She had more jiggers in her feet than any other little one I had known, because she received almost no care in her home. Living with her grandmother and step-grandfather, she tried to smile, but her life was very difficult.

Lovista had a horrible childhood, which she could not even talk about for years after she came to live with us. I learned that the step-grandfather would drink too much and then severely abuse her while drunk. Lovista slept in the so-called kitchen with the goats, but when I tried to take her home with me, the grandmother would not let her go. She said she needed her to help at home and often did not send her to school. Lovista carried water and worked in the gardens, but her grandmother fed her very little, so she often came to my home for something to eat and drink. After some time, I got a court order to remove her from that home and place her with a different relative.

There was a time when Lovista wanted to give up. She thought no one cared or loved her. She wanted to end her life and almost committed suicide. Going through so much and being shifted all over was hard on this young girl who had never experienced joy or the goodness of life. She found Christ in Scripture Union, a club at school, in her later years of high school and has become an "Overcomer," as Mandisa (American gospel singer) would sing. She did not overcome alone, she overcame through Christ, and she is not going under.

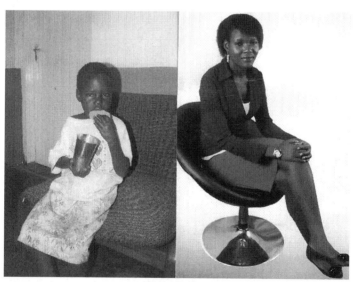

Mangi Lovista

Lovista received much counseling, which enabled her to become a wonderful Christian lady who says Jesus helped her through the trials. She graduated from Nkuma University in 2015 and is now looking for the job she wants. She always has a beautiful smile on her face and the love of Christ is reflected in her. Lovista has learned that Jesus is always with us – His love is real and never ends, for He promised that he *will ask the Father, and he will give you another Counselor to be with you forever – the Spirit of truth. The world cannot accept him, because it neither sees him nor knows him. But you know him, for he lives with you and will be in you. I will not leave you as orphans; I will come to you* (John 14:16-18). Lovista has this promise that He will not harm her or do something wrong to her. He is her Savior and He is her Lord.

Violet's Siblings

Some of the children do not have as happy an ending as Lovista. Junior was a little boy who touched my life to the core. He was Violet's younger brother, but I did not meet him until he was seven years old. He, too, was Esther's son – the very same Esther who had come to Jesus and left her daughter with me had left Violet's two younger brothers, Junior and Derrick, with an uncle. Junior was three at the time and Derrick was one year old when Esther died.

Junior found me one day when I was looking for Violet who was nine years old and had been living with me for four and a half years already. When the uncle found out that Junior had AIDS, he brought him back to the village to stay with the grandfather to die. He also left Derrick with the grandfather, because he thought surely Derrick must have AIDS also. He no longer had any interest in raising them or helping them in any way, and Junior was devastated. When he came to Violet, she broke down in tears.

Violet discovered that the grandfather thought the best thing he could do for them was to starve them to death since they had AIDS and would probably die anyway. When they came to Violet, they were very hungry, and she would sneak food out to them. Finally, she broke down and told me what was happening. I could not believe that people could be so cruel, but they felt justified in trying to end their suffering. I wanted to take them in, but the grandfather told me that if they died, I would be blamed. So, I continued to help them from home.

Why? Why? Why? I felt so helpless. I cried out to God every evening for them. I took each of them for testing so I would know how sick they were and discovered that Derrick did not have AIDS at all. Once he started getting food, he improved, and the uncle put him back in school.

Junior, however, was very sick with the virus and needed help. I got a court order to remove him from his grandfather's house and placed him with his grandmother on the other side of the family. The grandmother tried to care for him, but it seemed we were too late. Junior could not keep food down, and the medicine was too strong to take without food, so everything he ate came back up.

I was with him the last night before he died. I brought a mild soup that he was able to keep down and sat with him. I talked with him about Jesus, but he said Jesus did not love him and God had forgotten him and didn't care. I told him that was not true, that Jesus loved him very much. He kept shaking his head and saying, "No! How can you say this? Look at me. If He loved me, He would not let this happen to me. No one loves me but you." I told him that my love came from Jesus, and He had sent me there.

I told him that Jesus does love him, and these things happen in an imperfect world that was ruined by sin. I went through the whole story of the gospel with him, because we know that *faith comes from hearing the message, and the message is heard through the word of Christ* (Romans 10:17). He cried and said, "Pray with me that I can believe."

At about 11:00 p.m., I got ready to go home, and Junior put his arms around me and cried, "Don't leave me – please." He kept crying that he was going to die, and he didn't want to die alone. I told him that he was never alone because Jesus was always there.

I promised him I'd come back in the morning. He cried again, "No, stay please." But I had to return home. When I went back in the morning, I found him dead. I cannot describe what I felt that morning – to this day I cry for Junior and pray that the Lord took him home to be with him and love him.

Burying Junior was hard because the family did not want to help. They wanted to wrap him in a cloth and put him in the ground, but we buried him in a beautiful casket and gave him a good headstone. I cried and cried, asking God why, even though I knew God had reasons, it was hard to watch Violet suffer and cry silently. At the age of nine, she had already buried her father, her mother, and now her brother. Death has made it difficult for Violet to believe in the Lord, but the family was impacted by the love I had for this little boy.

Derrick is now in his last year of high school, and Violet is in the university. Their other brother Allan, who was sponsored, is working in Kampala in auto mechanics. Another sister was forced to marry a Muslim and convert to Islam. She escaped from him once to go to school, but they found her and beat her terribly. I could do nothing for her but pray.

These children have suffered, and I could not take away the pain they felt though I cried to God many times. All things are in His time. Violet stays in my home to this day and now believes and loves the Lord Jesus Christ. She is still very quiet and told me that she still needs a lot of healing, but she trusts the Lord to help her now instead of depending on others. She is in her last year of studies at Makerere University School of Business as she studies accounting.

Violet today

The Little Boy

Benard was three years old and not ready for school when we found a sponsor for him in the ministry. His mother was a skeptical lady who took a lot of persuasion to convince her to come to church and the women's Bible study. She trusted in witch doctors to solve her problems, and her husband drank a lot and was often not around. His job took him away, and he drank his money up before he came home.

Benard liked Sunday school and singing songs, and this sweet little boy was happiest when his mother came to church. Within six months, he was lucky to get a sponsor, but tragedy struck after six more months. Benard was in the gardens tending the goats, while his mother was digging. He did not see it! A snake. A deadly king cobra. He backed up while watching the goat, and the snake bit him. The poor mother did not know what to do, and she cried and killed the snake with a large stick.

She picked Benard up and started to carry him to the clinic where Margaret was working but could not manage as she was pregnant and it was too far. She proceeded to have Benard walk even though the bite was in the ankle/heel area. He died before they reached the clinic. The mother was heartbroken and blamed God, because she could not understand why He would take her child.

Unfortunately, Benard's is a story of what happens sometimes, and we cannot answer the question of why. To this day his mother will not come back to church, and though God has given her four other children, two boys and two girls, she is still bitter. We continue to pray for her and share with her whenever we get a chance. I found her one day at the home of a witch doctor where she had gone to get help.

Sometimes people approach the ministry in a misguided way. As long as they are being helped and things go the way they think they should, they are happy, go to church, and seem to be Christians. But in truth, they do not always know the Lord, and when something goes wrong, their faith is the first thing that goes. Whether they truly believed or not, only God knows.

I have learned that God is always there, even when I felt He was not. He is hearing and seeing all that goes on around me. We cannot do it alone; we must help one another draw near to Jesus and learn to be humble and joyful. The path of tears and trials makes us more like Jesus and humbles us to where God can use us.

Boney and Siblings

Three other children lived in a home where the parents brewed liquor every day. These children lost their father to AIDS and their mothers (the father had two wives) were elsewhere with different husbands and had abandoned the children. They lived with the grandfather.

The house these children had been living in belonged to their father, but it collapsed during the rainy season. We started them in the sponsorship program when Mary was seven, Charles was nine, and Boney (his real name was Boniface) was ten years old, and they came to live in my home.

We worked on building another house for them but discovered the home environment was not good for the children. Witchcraft was being practiced in addition to the brewing and drinking of liquor every day.

Not long after the children came to my home, Charles and Boney's real mother died from AIDS in a hospital in Kampala. She had been married to a Muslim but came to Christ before she died. The husband refused a Christian burial, and once again, I was frustrated and unable to do anything about it. The boys thought she wouldn't go to heaven because her burial was not Christian, but I told them she had nothing to do with that and as long as she believed and had accepted Christ to live in her heart, she was saved.

Boney found life very difficult. He was a handsome young man as he grew but very confused and lost in his life. Even as a young boy, he was always getting into trouble. One time when he was in the seventh grade, he locked the teachers and all the children in his classroom, and then he put sticks under the door and made them think he was going to set it on fire. He said he would never kill anyone and that they were wrong in believing he would, because he was just teasing. I told him this was not a good way to tease and he had scared everyone in the classroom. He said the teacher had made him angry and embarrassed him when he was using the bathroom, so he wanted to get back at him by scaring him.

Boney continued to get into trouble at school. In high school he was suspended from one school because they said he set fire to the Headmaster's office. He finished school, however, and his grades were good. Boney was a very bright young man.

I came to understand Boney, even though few people did. Charles and Mary were very close to him because he had always looked out for them. People told him he was like his father and just as dangerous, but I didn't know this until he told me later.

Often I prayed with him and listened to him, and he always had excuses as to why he did something. But I knew for sure he had a tender heart.

Mom and boneface

I was never one to give up on a child, because I knew Jesus wouldn't. I hung in there for Boney, and I knew he looked to me as his mother. I miss the long talks and discussions we often had.

When Boney was twenty-one, he finished his computer classes in a university equivalent program and was about to start his internship, but he was killed in a motorcycle accident. He was taking people to and from an introduction for one of our employees. He had left to get his grandfather, but was going a little too fast. The motorcycle slipped in the gravel, and he went flying into the ditch. He had many injuries but seemed to be okay, so I left for Kenya. I received a call at five in the morning that my son was dead.

Burying a child is a hard thing to do, but the hardest part was not being sure Boney ever accepted Christ. He read his

Bible and told me he believed, but he always had a difficult time doing what he was supposed to be doing. However, even the apostle Paul shared that sin was at war in his body, making it a struggle to do what was right (Romans 7). We can rejoice in his words to the Ephesians: *For it is by grace you have been saved, through faith – and this not from yourselves, it is the gift of God – not by works, so that no one can boast* (Ephesians 2:8-9). Boney always asked for my prayers, so I prayed. We must never give up hope. I am thankful that our God never gives up on us.

At the funeral for Boney, a lady came forward with a nineteen-month-old girl named Mary. Apparently Boney had a secret wife in the traditional Ugandan way (not married, just living together), and they had a daughter that I never knew about. The lady wanted to know what I was going to do with Mary. What a shock! I was not sure how to answer this, because I was grieving the loss of my son and could not think about it at that time.

I later remembered Mary and found her living with Boney's uncle and aunt. I took her into my home when she was three and a half years old, and she has been a real joy to me, like her Aunt Mary.

More Children

I have raised sixteen children in my home and currently have ten children living with me. Each has a unique story of how they came to live in my home, and each has had their share of heartache and struggles. All but one have come to know Jesus as their Savior.

One son, Benjamin, left the Islamic religion when he was seventeen and became a Christian. Our Henry led him to the Lord, and both of them went to another African country to study the Bible for a year after high school. Today Henry works for us as a Project Manager of the craft center, and Benjamin is a doctor in a major hospital in Kampala. They do mission work together whenever possible. How exciting it is to see the Lord work in their lives and the lives of other children who have passed through our home.

Katherine's Kids, 2013>>

Andrew Bukoli – Andrew Bukoli today is twenty-four years old. He finished with a Bachelor's Degree in Business Administration/ Accounting at Nkumba University. He says that I have been a mother of all sorts to him and that God gave me a big heart and a spirit of love, care, forgiveness, and many other things. He says that I am a true missionary. He was born in a family of five children – three brothers and one sister, and he is the last born. His parents died in different years: his father died in 1996 and his mother in 1998. He became frustrated, desperate, and hopeless because he could not see light at the end of the tunnel. He could not think positive because he thought that was the end of everything.

Then one day, HUM came to his home and shared with his grandmother, who was now taking care of him and his siblings, and things began to change. He got a sponsor and this gave him hope. The missionary told him it was because of God helping him. He says he could not see God at that time, because of the troubles he had been through, not to mention the heartache.

Life began to change rapidly and ambitions began to crop up in his life. He began to dream and dream big. He began to see hope and destiny – it was all possible. He feels strong that in life we meet certain people, each one of them has something to offer, something new and new ideas. HUM changed his life through the love of Christ. It was not easy with nothing good to sleep on, let alone the starvation at times and poor health.

In his own words: After getting a sponsor, I began to go to church and to school. Hines ministries began to empower me spiritually through the AWANA program, church programs, and other activities that have instigated (encouraged) growth of this inner man, to keep him warm and alive. The education I have attained has connected me to different people with different personalities, people from different political, social, economic, and religious backgrounds. Without the education and God, my ambitions would have rotted with me in the village.

God sent Hines to help me. My life is different from what it would have been because of the sponsors and Hines, and more importantly, because I found Jesus in my life. Special thanks to my mom, Katherine, and the One Accord Class, and to my sponsors, who sponsored me financially and prayed for me. May the almighty God who sees what is done in secret reward them and bless them and their children.

Bumba Dison – Bumba graduated from Uganda Christian University with a Bachelor's Degree in Environmental Science. He currently works with the Hines Ugandan Ministries in their offices and helps with kids who are just like he was, while he is working on his Master's degree in the same university.

Bukoli Andrew

In his own words: I did not make it to the level I am by expectation, but I thank God that today I am doing my Master's degree in UCU and hope to one day work in government and make a difference in this country. I love Jesus and realize that all things have been possible because of Him, and I thank Him for sending Hines to this country and for the work the ministry does as a whole for other children like me.

My father died in 1997, when I was six years old. I was the youngest of eight children. My father's occupation was a farmer. We all lived together in one mud thatched hut. My mother could not do much to help me, because she was now a widow with no income, and she had no education to find work. She worked hard digging, however, and did her best to cater for my needs. Sometimes Dad and Mom would brew liquor and sell alcohol, and they would get very drunk. We used to be beaten, sleep hungry and sometimes at the neighbors' homes, delay to be taken to school and were neglected as children. We used to walk naked because no one would bother to get clothes for us.

For some time, we lived in utter poverty, worse than before his death, and my mother could do nothing. She mourned his death and revived her habit of brewing liquor. The hut we lived in would leak when it rained. We were hungry most of the time.

When Hines first came to our home for the first time in 1995, she shared the gospel, and it was hard to listen to or believe then. I could see no future in my life. Our house wanted to cave in, and we only had the mud hut. I watched cattle most of the time with David, who also had no life to look forward too. She came back and took David and left me. I thought she had forgotten me.

She then came back later in 1998 and took my picture and wrote down information, and then I got a sponsor in 1999. Wow, I did not know my life would change so much. Even later as I went to school and began attending AWANA and church and learning more about Jesus, she said I did not know the plans He had for me were so good. In high school I gave my life to Christ and was so thankful for my sponsors. They even built me a small house and small latrine and then came back and helped me to help my mother have a better house. I saw that God was strong with them and I could dream again. I give thanks to God for all He has provided and all that He has done for me and my mother and David.

I enjoy working in the ministry and helping other children and seeing them change too, as I did with the help of God. It is humbling and always reminds me of where I started and came from.

Simon Maiso – in his own words: My name is Simon and I lost my father in 1999. I remained with my widowed mother, and she was a very poor woman. She never studied and had no job, income or any way to help us. She was also sick and was a peasant farmer who could not earn much. She was a Catholic and could not teach us about Jesus Christ, so I knew less about God and the Bible at large. She later died in 2002.

When I got sponsored by HUM in November 1999, I began learning about God through the AWANA program on Saturday and Sunday school at church. We even had seminars and workshops, and Momma Katherine herself would come and share in our home. Having a sponsor, I was sent to school and had a chance that my parents never had or even my older brother. I never expected to study even from the cheapest schools in my country because I didn't have any source of income. I thank the Lord for the sponsors through Hines and the workers for being faithful and loving and seeing me through. They even constructed a home for me and two of my brothers to live in where we had two bedrooms, a sitting area, kitchen, and an outhouse. We never had a bathroom before or anything like a bedroom. We had always lived in a one room hut altogether.

The ministry and Momma cared more about our life even through feeding and medical needs, not just education, and even more about our spiritual needs. I completed my education with a Bachelor's Degree from Nkumba University in Procurement and am working now in Kampala area. I am so thankful for all God has done through my life through Momma Katherine and Hines Ugandan Ministries and the workers there.

Norah Kisakye – in her words: I am Norah Kisakye and am twenty-two years, being born in 1993. I will be twenty-three this year. I was born in a village area called Sekulo having two brothers and five sisters. One of my brothers died from AIDS, and it is this brother that I had lived with for some time after both parents had died.

I am an orphan who lost both of my parents when I was two months old. I ended up with my oldest brother and went to nursery school when I was four years old. My oldest brother was married, and I was the youngest of the eight children. After three years of schooling, I had to stop due to things not going well in my brother's and his wife's lives. Poverty became an issue, and I wondered what changed. I started working, cleaning house for my sister-in-law and could do all the work alone.

Time reached when all the hope I had was gone, because even all the biggest sisters I had were struggling. They stayed in the house where my parents had lived and had no income. They were struggling to find ways to go to school now and then.

At seven years old, I had to look for food from the streets of Kampala because I was no longer given food at home. I did this for seven months. Then my brother passed away and his wife could not afford to keep me. I was then not sure what to do. Then my sister Judith met Pastor Charles Magale, and she was working for Hines Ugandan Ministries. She was making enough to take herself to school and going to get married. When she got married, her husband welcomed me to come and live in their home. He called me his first daughter. I was now ten years old.

Shortly after this, I got a sponsor through Hines and was taken to the best high school. Now I am working on an internship for two years at the Holmes Medical Center as a nurse. I am still studying with another two years to go for my diploma in comprehensive nursing. I know that God has looked out for me and heard my cries and prayers.

Pastor Charles and my sister, Judith, became more than a sister to me, but they became like parents. I am really thankful that God has taken such good care of me. Mom Katherine is like an Aunt that I can only dream of. She has also been there for me. I know that God is with me now and He cares for me, and I can see now that He always was with me.

Harriet Konga – in her words: I am Harriet Konga, born in

Nyanza Village, which is part of Kamonkoli. I come from the family of the late Nyaiti, and my mother's name is Zebulence. My father died in 1992 when I was only five years old. I was living with my mother who was only a housewife with no education. She could hardly provide all the basic needs without even thinking about school needs.

By God's grace, however, in 1998 I got saved. That is when I was in primary three. Still, my education was left in the hands of God because my mother had no hope of educating me any further. God is so precious that as I was in primary four in November 1999, I got a sponsor through Hines Ugandan Ministries. They started paying my school fees and all other basic requirements as I was staying with my mother until 2006. In 2006 I started staying with Aunt Christine who worked for Mom Katherine in the ministry. Aunt Christine always ate her meals in Mom Katherine's home, and I now became a member of this home.

They even took me to a good school and put me through all of my primary school, high school, and through university. I went to Kyambogo University in Kampala and graduated with my Bachelor's Degree in Economics. I graduated on February 20, 2014. I am so grateful to God for He has done much for me in my life, and great thanks to His servant Hines and the entire staff, with special thanks to Mom Katherine and Aunt Christine. May God bless them so much and my sponsors who were faithful to sponsor me all the way through. My life is a living testimony to God for the love I have been given through Jesus.

Mary Nanyonga – in her words: My name is Mary Nanyonga, and I was born on the 18th of April in 1994. My father died of AIDS when I was only two years old, and that was in 1996. After my father's death, my mother had to leave me behind with my grandfather and grandmother who were so poor and could not afford taking care of me. My two brothers, Charles and Boney, were trying to help in taking care of me. Their mother was there and tried to help, but she died soon after.

Then my grandmother fell sick and eventually died. Her death left me in deep pain and sorrow, because I never, at any one moment, thought she would die and depart us just like that. I did not know the person who would really take care of me and my brothers. After her death, life was never the same. Getting something to eat was not a joke. Every morning we could go out and dig so that we could get some little money to feed ourselves. Grandfather would not give us food unless we did digging. Despite the fact that she had died, the house we were staying in was in a very bad condition, and it finally crashed in. It was raining really hard when it caved in, and it was scary because we were sleeping.

Before my grandmother's death, however, she had gone and registered us for sponsorship in Hines Ugandan Ministries. When Mom Katherine came to find out about what we were going through, she started paying for us to eat our meals in a nearby restaurant for lunch, and on the weekends eating at her home and staying with her. Life at my grandfather's home was impossible, and this is when Mom Katherine took us in and became like a real mother to us.

I am what I am today simply because of God's grace and Hines Ugandan Ministries. I was once that kid who was so hopeless, full of pain and sorrow. I never knew that life would change as it did. I am now in Kyambogo University studying Economics and Finance. I am looking forward to where God will take me next. I believe that God, who has been seeing me through, will still use me and see me through until my life here is done. I appreciate all that God has done, Mom Katherine, Aunt Christine, Pastor Charles, and the entire staff, and I appreciate my sponsors who have shown me love too. I am what I am today because they cared.

Beatrice Sarah Sabano – in her words: I am Sabano Beatrice Sarah, born on 28th of August 1986. I am the second born out of eight children in my family. Life was not easy for me. I was living in a critical condition with both parents, whereby I had one dress and one pantie in my life. I used to stay with both parents. My father had a problem with drinking. He used to stay in bars drinking all the time and using all his money on beer and ladies. No support was at home. My mother was a peasant, and we used to work in people's gardens to get something to eat and get some money for medical needs.

One day when I decided to take Jesus Christ as my Savior in my life in the 5th grade in 1998 July, it was the beginning of my suffering terrible pain in my life. My father denied me, that I was not his daughter. He used to call me stupid, and whenever he was back from drinking in the evening, he would cane me and said he would kill me for being saved in his family. He abused me terribly.

My life was very, very, hard and painful for me. I attended school without books, no lunch, and no uniform. I used to borrow papers to write my notes on from friends. Until 2000, when I came to know about Hines Ugandan Ministries through my friend, Diana, who was staying with Katherine. Mom Katherine started helping me with books and uniform and other materials needed. Still my parents refused me to attend church and AWANA on Saturdays. I started escaping from home to go to church on Sundays. When my mother came to know what was going on, she used to take me to the garden on Sundays and give me a big portion to dig so that I would not have time to go, because the work was too much. I cried a lot over this.

Then in 2001, I got sponsorship, and my life began to change completely. I started being happy again, having a smile on my face unlike before. I was now having a lunch at school, a new uniform, and my own books, shoes, pens, pencils, math set, school bag, and clothes for the first time in my life. I started attending church and AWANA freely without much difficulties like before. Hines played a very big role in my life.

I went to live with Mom Katherine in 2001. Then my father got saved in 2004, because I continued to go and share with him whether he like it or not. My mother also started coming to church, and she gave her life to Christ as well. I really give thanks to God for all of this.

I moved on through high school and did well. Mom Katherine had me sent to university at Uganda Christian University, and I got my diploma in Social Work. Later, after working for Hines, I went back and got my Bachelor Degree in Social Work Administration. I now get to serve the children here that are like me and others that are in pain and sorrow and suffering so much. I praise God so much for letting me work to serve Him and all that He does for me. I know that He is using me to make an impact too.

Alpha Namuyanja – in her words: My name is Namuyanja Alpha, and I am from a polygamous family. I am the fourteenth out of fifteen children. Four of these fifteen children have died and passed on. My father had more than one wife in life, and it was not easy staying with stepmothers. They could mistreat us whenever Dad was not around or if my mother was not around. My mother is a hairdresser and sometimes helps with assistant teaching in a primary school. She met Mom Katherine at the school when she was working. She also had a client that worked for Mom Katherine, and she came and told her where to find her. My father died and then I was taken to Mom Katherine's because my mother was also sick with the dreaded illness (AIDS). I found Mom Katherine and some other little girls like me there and some boys too. They all showed me love and care, and I felt so much at home. Mom Katherine allowed me to be coming over every weekend. I would come on Friday evenings so that I did not miss AWANA on Saturdays.

The situation in my home got worse because it was a Muslim home. I was only five years old when my father passed away, and the other siblings and family were against me because I talked of Christian things. I always had support from my mother though because she had become a Christian. Later my two sisters accepted Christ. I began to pray for God to do something in my life. Then Mom Katherine found me a sponsor, and she took me in to stay with her. This was in the fifth grade, and I was happy and thanked God. The Sponsorship program has not only strengthened my relationship with Christ, but also catered for my needs and studies, and even clothes and shoes.

I want to take the opportunity to appreciate all that the program has done for me and is doing for me. I am currently attending Makerere School of Business and studying accounting. The almighty God is to be thanked above all, and I pray that one time I can reach out to other children who were like me and help them in this world. In God I trust now.

The late **Samuel Okwera** – in his words: I was born on 2nd December 1996. My father passed away when I was six months old. After my father's death, my mother left me with my grandmother, and she never came back, although she came to visit when I was five years old but still stayed away. In 1998, I was joined by Hines Ugandan Ministries, and they started supporting me and helping me, even though I was sickly all the time. Despite the fact that I was to the hospital, nothing really changed, and I kept on wondering what the problem was that I had to be taken to the hospital in the first place. Since my mother was infected with HIV/AIDS and my father had died from this, I was advised by my grandmother to take a test, and it turned out to be that I was also infected. I could not believe it because I thought that it was only my mother and father who had it. She just told me to be strong and she encouraged me. However, I started taking the ARV drugs for the sickness and simply knew I had to do this for the rest of my life.

In 2012 my grandmother passed away. She was like the only family I had besides my younger cousin brother, Francis Wabwire. Despite the hard times I went through, I got some encouragement from Mom Katherine and Aunt Nancy in the ministry. Life was too hard for me though. I was always feeling sick.

I am really thankful to Hines Ugandan Ministries for helping me and for rendering me this far. It is by the grace of God that I am still standing. I do not know what would have happened to me. It enabled me to attain my education, at least to see a brighter future ahead of me. The ministry has helped me build a spiritual life in Christ and may the glory and honor go to the Lord Almighty.

Update: Samuel passed away in 2014 when he became too sick to fight the illness that was attacking him. His defenses were down after his grandmother died, and the care he received was not the same after she died. Though he often got help from Mom Katherine, Nancy, Christine, and Pastor Charles, he could not make it. He became very depressed after his grandmother's death, and he continued to become more depressed as the sickness increased. He contracted malaria and typhoid, and he could not manage to fight it. I believe that Samuel is with our Lord Jesus Christ, as he did accept Him and believe in Him in his life.

Nathan Wozere – in his words: I always gasp in disbelief whenever I remember how God saved me from dying during my birth. Really God did it for me. It was on one hazy morning when all the birds were chirping over the whirling trees all over. Pain waved through my mother as she thought of visiting Budadiri Hospital for a health checkup. Upon waiting for the results, the poor lady was informed that she could not push the baby. This was because I was in a bad position, holding one hand between my legs, according to the x-ray.

The only way to save me was through surgery with a C-section. She went to Mbale hospital and I arrived after the surgery. A successful operation was achieved by God's grace, and I was removed when I was lacking enough oxygen. Without moments delay, the doctors took me to an oxygen room and placed me in an oxygen mask. Mum was kept in the surgical ward, being treated while I was kept in an oxygen mask. All this happened the way that God planned it, and He loved me.

I grew up knowing that I had no father until I was twelve years old. Then Mum thought to tell me about my father and took me to meet him. We went to Budaka to see my dad on a day blazing with the azure in the sky as though Jesus was coming back.

Upon our arrival, silence reigned over the home, as everyone was eager to receive us. However, as you know – whatever glistens is not gold! We found there a stepmother and a big snake known as a python. There was a crocodile as well. My stepmother decided to just hate me. She made my father decide not to like me either. He did not care about our needs. It must have been God who provided us with meals in those days without our knowing.

We lived in a grass-thatched hut with many openings on the roof that allowed the rain in whenever it was rainy. I grew up knowing plastic bags as my comfy bed, because it was all I had to sleep on, and mum would give me one of her two dresses to cover with if it was cool. Dad did not care about our existence, our suffering, or how we lived. Whatever we got from working, he took away and gave it to the stepmother. It hurt me as a child and still does.

I will leave you son, my mother would say and thought of it daily because she was extremely tired of the situation of harassment and all that went on. My dad and my stepmother practiced witchcraft on a regular basis, and that is why they had a python in one shrine and a crocodile in another.

My mum continued to work hard daily to see that I could eat, and she would hide some of the money. She then began purchasing some building materials somewhere else, so that we could have a shelter for ourselves. We still live in this room to this day.

When I reached the 6th grade, I saw the impossibility of finishing through the 7th grade because of buying uniforms, pens, and pencils. It was all becoming too much burden. God, I need your support, I would pray. I prayed to Him even when I could not remember the last time I was in church.

Then one day He answered my prayers when I went to the Presbyterian church where the muzungu went. I met Mom Katherine and she took interest in my life. I felt it was God that led me to the ministry. Hines Ugandan Ministries then got me a sponsor, and my life has changed drastically. Thank you, Jesus, my Lord, and may God bless Hines.

Ivan Nyaiti – in his own words: Glory be to the living almighty God who is the creator of the heavens and the earth. For the great things He has done in my life from the day I was born to the man that I am now living. It has not been a simple journey, only but the grace of God am I here.

When I was born, after sometime, my parents left me with my grandmother, and they went away from where I was left. My grandmother was a widow, and she had many children of her own that were not grown up yet. She managed somehow to care for me until I grew up.

When I started going to school, I had no one to help with school fees, books, etc., and I was taken to be in a village school from the 1st grade in 2004, where my grandmother struggled to find me materials to help me go to school. Sometimes an uncle would help and give me some books or pens or pencils.

When I started understanding life, my grandmother took me to have a picture taken and get a sponsor with Hines Ugandan Ministries. I was seriously struggling. There were many children wanting sponsors from Hines, and I had to trust God to bring me a sponsor. My grandmother just kept saying, "be patient."

Then when I was in the 5th grade, I got a sponsor and was happy to be a part of Hines Ugandan Ministries. I enjoyed AWANA because they talked of God so much. I completed my primary studies very well in 2011 and was enrolled in high school. I was given all that I needed for school, or medical treatment, and even some food was given to us at home, clothes, shoes, and soap, etc. I was even given goats. I continued with my life and trusted in God again and again and even received a bicycle from my sponsor.

Hines has done great things in my life because whatever I need in life, they provide for me and they always make sure I don't live a miserable life. Not to think about the neglect of my parents, but they guided me to forgive them and have taught me more about God and how to live as a Christian.

I have passed through many challenges and difficult times, temptation, mistreatments, but I have been able to withstand all these because of the hope that I have in Christ.

Because of the great things God has done in my life, using Hines Ugandan Ministries, I have always decided to give my life to Him completely. Children leave school because of a lack of school fees. Some die from lack of food or treatment when sick. Some are on the streets begging for food, but I have been taken care of because God chose me and gave me help.

I am a person who was laughed at, a person who was abandoned, a person that meant nothing to anyone (besides my grandmother). I am now a child of the most high God who has had grace and given me life forever. I am at a level in high school that God brought me to and is continuing to bless me each and every day and in everything I do.

Though I still stay with my widowed grandmother, I am becoming a young man who has been changed and has hope and a future because of God and the parents he gave me through Hines Ugandan Ministries. The staff and Mom Katherine have been like real parents to me. They have taught me how to share the gospel, how to speak even to the congregation, and encouraged me in a gift that the Lord has given me in preaching His word. I have become the chairperson of the Scripture Union in the high school where I go, and all this is because the Lord loves me. To God alone the glory for great things He has done in my life.

David Munyangha – in his words: My name is Munyangha David. I joined the Hines Ugandan Ministries in 2002 after my father had passed on and my mother could not fully facilitate me in any school or even in the normal necessities of life. When I finished the 7th grade, I had done well and wanted to go on to high school, and it was then that I was welcomed by Judith on staff and given a chance to become a sponsored kid. Due to the grace of the Lord and the love that the administration felt for me and my widowed mother, I was told to prepare to go to school for high school.

In 2006 I was asked if I wanted to help with organizing an evangelistic crusade. During this crusade, I was touched by the message and accepted Jesus as my Lord and Savior. I continued going to high school. Mom Katherine and Aunt Christine, Pastor Charles and Judith paid for my rent and gave me food to eat, so that I could go to Kamonkoli College (which did not have boarding for boys). I became very sick at one point and had to be taken to Mbale General Clinic in Mbale town, where I was treated and became well. The ministry made sure that I received proper treatment.

I did my final examination in 2009 for the 4th year of high school and the end of the ordinary level and did well. I stood during my holiday time as a youth participant in the church activities. In 2010, because I had passed well, I was admitted to Bugwere High School to do my advance level of high school, and then I went on to get my degree is secondary education at Uganda Christian University.

More than all of this – with education and all, I have life to the fullest, because I found the Lord. The ministry and church have helped me to grow spiritually and morally upright in the Word and has taught me the importance of loving others.

Allow me to appreciate the people of Kamonkoli. More so the Mulonde family for cooperating with Hines Ugandan Ministries and helping Hines when she first came, and the ministry as a whole for all they do to help the children and youth in Kamonkoli. We are thankful to God the Almighty who gave Hines a dream and brought her to come and love the people here in Kamonkoli, and all the whites that come to visit us and care.

I have spiritual transformation in my life, have learned to be responsible and care for myself and one day a family, good health, and love and care from parents that are part of the ministry. More than any of this, salvation is mine, and our beloved Pastor Charles and Mom Katherine have shared the Word over and over, and lives are changed through the seeds they plant. I am thankful to be passing on with the Word too and sharing and planting seeds now too.

The Stories

So many stories – I cannot tell them all because nearly two hundred children have finished this program. Most of them know the Lord, but not all of them live for Him. They know the truth but do not realize it can change their lives forever because they have not opened their hearts, like so many people in the world today.

I praise the Lord that He has used me and the staff here at HUM to make a difference in many lives – to educate children, help them to be healthier and have better hygiene, and understand so many things. Most important is that they know who Christ is and what He has done for them.

One of the biggest rewards is seeing the ones who are in Christ reaching out to other children and people around them with that same love and care they received, wanting to see others know Him and have changed lives too.

Chapter Twenty

Bringing Hope

*Command those who are rich in this present world
not to be arrogant nor to put their hope in wealth,
which is so uncertain, but to put their hope in God,
who richly provides us with everything for our
enjoyment.* 1 Timothy 6:17

Mother Theresa said we should love until it hurts and
then love some more. I often hurt and feel the pain of
the Ugandan people and children. Jesus said, *Let the little children come to me, and do not hinder them, for the kingdom of
God belongs to such as these* (Luke 18:16). The Lord impressed
upon my heart how much they need love and care. Real love and
care – unconditional love and care that they would find through
Jesus. Uganda did not need another sponsorship program but
a real caring and loving sponsorship program.

What does this love look like? If one is thirsty, love looks like
clean water. If one is hungry, love may look like a piece of bread.
If one is hurting, love may be a hug or a smile or an encouraging word. People need to know they are loved by Jesus before

they can love others. *We love because He first loved us* (1 John 4:19). We are loved with an unconditional love. Jesus knows all of us by name and by every hair on our head, yet He loves us. Paul tells us in Romans 5:8 that *God demonstrates his own love for us in this: While we were still sinners, Christ died for us.*

Watching children grow and change over the years and become responsible young adults has been the greatest experience I could ever have. Loving like Jesus did is embracing the suffering as he did. Love perseveres in any language and brings hope to those who have none.

We bring the message of hope to these children and the people in this village and other villages where we now have children sponsored. This hope comes through the gospel of Jesus Christ by ministering to the spiritual, physical, and practical needs of orphans and children at risk, as well as widows. We pour out love and compassion on all of them, because *those who hope in the Lord will renew their strength. They will soar on wings like eagles; they will run and not grow weary, they will walk and not be faint* (Isaiah 40:31).

I have seen many children die, and I will never be able to put the dying moments of some out of my mind. I have watched many adults die, and funerals take place nearly every week, sometimes many. Every day, I find out that another person who has children has AIDS. Uganda is a country where 51 percent of the total population of thirty-eight million are under the age of fifteen, and 77 percent are under the age of twenty-two.

In this war-torn country that is stricken with disease and poverty, people need love and hope more than ever. This hope can only come through Jesus Christ in their lives. As we see lives changed and given hope, we can only praise our Lord who is making it possible through us.

I am excited when I see my children – God's children – grown up and preaching the gospel, so others may know Him. I trust

God's Word in Proverbs 22:6, which says *train a child in the way he should go, and when he is old he will not turn from it.* I praise God when they tell me they are going to sponsor a child when they are working. I praise God when they lead worship, Bible study, or work in a crusade or outreach, as it is a joyful and wonderful moment that gives God glory.

I dislike going home to the United States to raise funds because I have to leave my children. One time when I was away for six months, I called to talk to the children at home, and little Goma, who was three years old at the time, said to me, "Momma, I am going to be sick until you come home!" I cried for hours; I just wanted to hug him and hold him and tell him that I loved him.

I do enjoy seeing my friends and meeting new people, and I know how important it is to get funds to help these children. I have come to realize, however, that I no longer fit in on the American soil. I don't live in that world any longer, where everything looks cleaner, brighter, richer, and bigger, but it is no longer home to me even though I love many people in the United States. *I am a stranger to my brothers, an alien to my own mother's sons* (Psalm 69:8). My children make my home in Uganda and have become my family.

Even though we had very humble beginnings with nine child sponsors, our sponsorship program has grown by serving the children and giving God the glory. Today we have 242 in the program, and the number grows as we are able to adequately provide for them.

Our AWANA program is expanding with more and more children excited about God's Word. When they successfully recite the verse for the week, they receive a piece of candy. Watching their eyes light up and dark faces grin is thrilling to see. Knowing they have the benefit of both candy and spiritual knowledge brings joy to me – and hope for them.

Sponsored Child receiving food

Richard Joan Margaret

Lunguba David

Bumba Dison and myself giving a goat to a child in need

Benjamin's Graduation 2016

In addition to the AWANA program, craft center, and sponsorship, we are excited to have our new clinic. It has two recovery rooms, an isolation/minor surgery room, a complete lab, two exam rooms, bathrooms, and a large waiting room.

Holmes Medical Clinic and Staff

Above all, we work to educate these children to give them a new direction in their lives here and an eternal home in the future. Our desire is to give these students the tools they need to be productive individuals wherever they live.

Recently we hired a new Head Master for our Genesis Primary School – Benard Eriradi Buddi. Education was instrumental in changing his life, and he wants many children to have the same opportunity that he had. In his own words:

"For three years, I was left at home, looking after goats because my family did not have the funds to send me to school past the seventh grade. I worked with an old man named Yokosofati. One day while we endured a great rainstorm, Yokosofati shared his life experiences with me. The next morning Yokosofati came to me and prayed for me concerning me going back to school. He said that if God wills for you to go to school, you will.

"Then another friend of Yokosofati's came and asked me if I would go to school if given the chance. When I said yes, he went away. Upon returning, he had a turkey and said I should sell it to help me get started with school. I sold it for about six dollars and went to a cheap school. The Headmistress agreed to let me start, and she would see if my performance was adequate. On my way home that evening, I found Yokosofati and told him everything. He gave me a pen to use at school.

"All of this was a beginning, and I learned more about Jesus and how he cares for us. I learned that he provides in strange ways. Later that year I came to accept him as my Lord and Savior, putting my trust in the Lord and realizing a personal relationship with Jesus Christ. He was faithful in helping me to get where I am today – in charge of a Primary School for Hines Ugandan Ministries." And, it all began with a turkey.

Chapter Twenty-One

Rescued Lives

*Religion that God our Father accepts as pure and
faultless is this: to look after orphans and widows in
their distress and to keep oneself from being polluted
by the world.* James 1:27

Some of the children who grew up in our program and school
are now able to work alongside Christine who is our
Sponsorship Administrator. Pastor Charles serves as our
Assistant Director, and his wife Judith helps Christine in Child
Sponsorship. Others work and serve the Lord in other areas.

It takes many dedicated, loving Christians to reach individuals for Christ and have an impact on their lives. Recently, I had
to deal with one of our sons (I'll call him Kenny). Kenny had
been struggling for a long time in school – and in life. He has
had a very rough life but was in his third year of high school
with passing grades in all of his classes when he was expelled
for taking drugs. The other eight boys who were involved were
put in prison, but the Headmaster knew the work we were doing
and let Kenny off.

Katherine and Christine 2015

My heart was breaking as I asked Kenny why he was doing this, "Don't you know it makes our Lord sad? God loves you and wants you to have a good life."

Then I shared from the Bible about living a life above reproach. I reminded Kenny that Christ died on the cross for him, so he could have eternal life. We talked about John 3:1-8:

> *Now there was a man of the Pharisees named Nicodemus, a member of the Jewish ruling council. He came to Jesus at night and said, "Rabbi, we know you are a teacher who has come from God. For no one could perform the miraculous signs you are doing if God were not with him"*

> *In reply Jesus declared, "I tell you the truth, no one can see the kingdom of God unless he is born again."*

"How can a man be born when he is old?"
Nicodemus asked. "Surely he cannot enter a second
time into his mother's womb to be born!"

Jesus answered, "I tell you the truth, no one can
enter the kingdom of God unless he is born of water
and the Spirit. Flesh gives birth to flesh, but the
Spirit gives birth to spirit. You should not be sur-
prised at my saying. 'You must be born again' The
wind blows wherever it pleases. You hear its sound,
but you cannot tell where it comes from or where it
is going. So it is with everyone born of the Spirit."

Then I shared Romans 3:23 with him: *For all have sinned and fall short of the glory of God*, and then Romans 6:23 which says, *For the wages of sin is death, but the gift of God is eternal life in Christ Jesus our Lord.*

After this we looked at Romans 10:9-10 which tells us *that if you confess with your mouth, "Jesus is Lord," and believe in your heart that God raised him from the dead, you will be saved. For it is with your heart that you believe and are justified, and it is with your mouth that you confess and are saved.* We talked about confessing and believing and went back to John 3:16, *For God so loved the world that he gave his one and only Son, that whoever believes in him shall not perish but have eternal life.*

Finally, we looked at 1 John 5:11-12 together: *And this is the testimony: God has given us eternal life, and this life is in his Son. He who has the Son has life; he who does not have the Son of God does not have life.* I wanted to be sure Kenny understood these basic truths.

Our God is a powerful and loving God and he has given us His powerful Word to strengthen and save us. He delivered Stephen, Jonah, and Florence from the clutches of the Devil and witchcraft. He lifts the desperate and dejected from the depths of despair to the heights of His glory.

Diana, Christine's little sister, is married today to Chris, a Christian American, and they live in the United States with their three children and operate their own business.

Julius is enjoying his work in the Middle East with the U.S. Troops.

Lovista, who was abused by her step-grandfather and slept in the kitchen with the goats, has received counseling. She studies travel and tourism at the university and will graduate in 2016 as a fine Christian lady.

Though Boney died in a motorcycle accident, his brother and sister thrived in a sponsorship program. Charles is studying to be a dentist, and Mary is studying finance and accounting.

Derrick has finished his last year of high school and is looking at vocational studies in information technology, and his brother Allan is working in Kampala in auto mechanics.

Violet, the little girl who broke the glass, has remained faithful. The shattered life was made whole by the only one who could work the miracle – God. She is in the university now.

Last to be mentioned is David – that one little boy with eyes filled with hopelessness who became one boy, all grown up, with eyes filled with hope and love. He studied Information Technology and Computer Science, has graduated from Makerere University in Kampala, and works as an Immigration Officer for the government. In his spare time, he builds websites. He has hope for his future, which brings hope for others. *Hope deferred makes the heart sick, but a longing fulfilled is a tree of life* (Proverbs 13:12). May we bring hope to many, many more.

More than 60 percent of our sponsorship program graduates are working and about 80 percent of them have come to Christ. I pray many more will do so in the future. To God be the glory – great things He has done.

Uganda – The Land of Paradoxes

Yes, Uganda is a land of paradox – so much contradiction, so little security. All of my trials shaped me for the triumph of God's glory in Uganda where grief resides with joy, as death resides with life. Playful children climb mango trees – but they are climbing for mangoes to stave off hunger or possibly starvation. The filth of the slums looms near the luscious tea plantations and sugar cane fields. The horror of the body parts floating in Lake Victoria next to the sublime magnificence of Mt. Elgon behind Wanale Mountain. But the miracle is when the hopelessness of poverty turns into the riches of eternal life in Jesus Christ with all of His hope and love – turning tragedies into triumph and bringing glory to God.

Epilogue

After the sponsorship program was going on well, I looked at the living conditions of the children.

The people are living in the dirt – sleeping in the dirt, eating in the dirt, bathing in the dirt and it is all they know. They live in mud huts where they smear cow dung to make the floor hard and kill any other bugs that may bite them in the evenings, such as ants. When I mentioned that the cow dung was not very clean and probably full of bacteria, they told me I was wrong and it was the best thing. I could not fathom this!

I designed a small home for these children to live in a healthier environment. It was a two bedroom house with a small cement bathroom that could be used for bathing – a cement slab with a hole to the outside with a strainer on it to keep bugs and other things from crawling up. The house also had a sitting room and small kitchen. In the beginning we built these houses for $5,000, and this would include a latrine or outhouse for toilets. I was surprised at how many donors were excited about this idea. We built eighteen of these homes around the village before stopping to work on the orphanage project.

Small housing project

We learned the hard way, however, that the small houses should have had more money invested to make sturdier foundations. The houses are still functioning, however, and make a difference in the lives of the people we place in them. People asked how we decided who should get these homes. We did not decide. We prayed, and it was up to the donors. However, to many Americans that was too much to spend, and now those houses cost about $20,000 because of the prices today.

Another Clinic

Over time I realized that if I was to have access to a clinic, it would need to be owned by the ministry. The one we had built really belongs to Margaret, and we let her run it as she wants. She still runs it very well, and we have been thankful for all the people it has served and still serves in the community.

However, we drew up plans that included a second clinic in a different area where the HUM property was purchased. Today we have this clinic, and it is known as Holmes Medical Clinic. We are thankful to the donors of this clinic and for the fact that it has a full lab and services to provide for the needs of the area. Michael is running this clinic, and we are excited about being able to help our children there.

The Vision Grows

As time went on, I knew we were helping many children, but as we grew, it was difficult to spend enough time with each child, making the difference we wanted to make, and laying a foundation. Simply meeting them on Saturdays in AWANA and Sundays at church was not enough. They were getting a lot of bad influence from their homes. Many of the children are in homes where there is polygamy, witchcraft, drinking, or all of these things.

I asked God to show me how I could have more influence with His Spirit in their lives to raise up godly leaders who will make a difference.

The answer came in the form of a primary (elementary) school. I realized that the schools were as bad of an influence as their homes, so I started Genesis Nursery/Primary School in 2011. Genesis – because it is the beginning and the laying of the foundation. I found a Christian curriculum to use together with the national curriculum.

It has not been easy, but today we have classes up to the 5th grade, including two nursery grades. Starting children when they are young and giving them Christ in everything, we can mold them with Christian values and thoughts from that young age. In this way, we can influence their lives more for Jesus.

We are still in the process of growing the school but have 180 students this year (2016) and will continue to grow as the Lord allows and provides.

Genesis kids showing off their work

Genesis Primary School

About the Author

Katherine has been a missionary in Uganda for over 20 years and has been working in a village called Kamonkoli. She has worked to make a difference in the lives of children and has seen many grow into strong Christian leaders. This is a girl who says she was a "Nobody" but to God she was "Somebody."

Connect with Katherine
www.hineskids.org

Other Similar Titles By

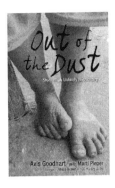

Avis Goodhart with Marti Pieper

"Don't waste your pain," says unlikely missionary Avis Goodhart. She didn't – and neither should you.

Despite a background of childhood abuse, dyslexia, and marital infidelity, Avis took her first international mission trip at age fifty. The church, school, and orphanage she later founded in northern Peru, all products of both her pain and her radical obedience to the Lord, have brought thousands of others out of the dust. This compelling story of an ordinary woman who serves God in extraordinary ways will challenge, inspire, and empower you to:

- Eliminate excuses from your life

- Recognize that in God's kingdom, availability matters more than ability

- Allow your pain to produce – not prevent – your obedience

- Serve the Lord with the same abandon shown by one unlikely missionary

Available where books are sold

Made in the USA
San Bernardino, CA
02 September 2017